LIFE

OF

SAINT DOMINIC

Defenfor · Fidei · Januæ · Ora · Pro · Nobis

S · DOMINIQUE

LIFE

OF

SAINT DOMINIC

BY THE

REV. PÈRE H.D. LACORDAIRE,

*Of the Order of St. Dominic, and Member
of the French Academy.*

TRANSLATED BY MRS. EDWARD HAZELAND.

ST. FRANCISVILLE
COR JESU PRESS
2023.

Published in 2023 by
Cor Jesu Press LLC
www.corjesupress.com

ISBN: 979-8-9891661-5-2

This edition has been re-typeset using the text of the 1883 edition entitled *Life of Saint Dominic* originally published by Burns and Oates.

Cover design by P.B. Fossier.

APPROBATION OF THE ORDER.

HAVING by command of the most Reverend Father Angelo Ancarini, Master-General of the Order of Friar Preachers, examined a book entitled *Vie de Saint Dominique, par le Révérend Père Henri Dominique Lacordaire, de l'Ordre des Frères Prêcheurs*, I declare that I have not found in it anything contrary to morals or faith. It is marked by great purity of style, correctness of thought, and by the golden eloquence and grace so characteristic of the writer. Therefore I consider that the publication of such a book would be a general boon, especially to France, in which country the Order of Friar Preachers was so useful and so flourishing in days gone by.

FR. TOMASO-GIACINTO CIPOLETTI,

Formerly Master-General of the Order of Friar Preachers, Theologian of La Casanate, Consultor of the Congregation of the Index, and of the Bishops and Regulars.

ROME, SANTA-MARIA-SOPRA-MINERVA,
  26th July 1840.

CONTENTS.

CHAPTER I.

CHAPTER II.

CHAPTER III.

CHAPTER IV.

CHAPTER V.

CHAPTER VI.

Contents.

Contents.

CHAPTER I.

Situation of the Church at the End of the Twelfth Century.

THE twelfth century of the Christian era dawned amid splendid auspices. The faith and the current ideas of the ages were in perfect harmony with each other; together they guided the West; out of a variety of races, at the same time obedient and free, they built up one single community. At the head of this vast social edifice was seated the Sovereign Pontiff, on a throne whence Majesty descended to succour Law, violated through human weakness, and Justice hastened to the succour of Obedience, the claims of which were rendered almost intolerable by the despotic abuse of power. Vicar of God and of man, Christ at his right hand and Europe at his left, the Roman Pontiff, weak in his own weakness but strong in divine strength, urged on the nations in the ways of righteousness. Never had faith, reason, and justice met together on so lofty a pedestal; never had the reunion of the severed members of the human race appeared so probable or so near. In Jerusalem, the banner of Christendom already waved over the Holy Sepulchre, and invited the Greek to a glorious reconciliation with the Latin Church. Islamism, defeated in Spain and chased from Italian shores, beheld itself attacked in the very stronghold of its power, and twenty nations, marching together to the frontiers of Christendom to defend the gospel of Christ from the pride of might and from the brutality of ignorance, promised Europe a cessation of those sanguinary migrations of which Asia was the home. Who could foretell the end of those triumphal ways just opened up by Christian chivalry in the East? Who foresee what the world might not become under a pontificate enabled to create, within, so vast a unity, without, so mighty an impulse?

But the twelfth century ended not as it had begun; and when, at eventide, it sunk beneath the horizon to rest in eternity, the Church too seemed to set, her brow overclouded by a gloomy future. No longer did the Cross of Jesus glitter on the minarets of the Holy City; our warriors, conquered by Saladin, retained but a few feet of Syrian soil; the Greek Church, instead of drawing nearer to the Church of Rome, had, by the ingratitude and perfidy evinced by her members to the Crusaders, become confirmed in schism. With the East all was over! Since then, history has demonstrated the consequences of that sad event: The fall of Constantinople; the occupation by Ottoman Turks of a portion of European territory; bitter slavery imposed on millions of Christians, and the whole of Christendom menaced by their arms until the time of Louis XIV.; the incursions of Tartars into the heart of Europe during three centuries; Russia adopting the Greek schism, and ready to descend on the West, to the destruction of liberty and law; Europe troubled by the downfall of the Mussulman races, even as she had been troubled by their ascendancy, and the partition of Asia become as difficult as her subjugation had formerly been. Montaigne says, "*Defeat is sometimes better than victory;*" and truly may we say that the nonsuccess of the plans conceived by Gregory VII. and his successors, with regard to the East, has revealed their genius far more clearly than the most victorious accomplishment of their designs could have done.

Within the Church the spectacle was no less sad. The efforts of St. Bernard to re-establish wholesome discipline had availed but little to stem the simony, luxury, and avarice of the clergy. The wealth of the Church, source of all the evils so eloquently depicted by St. Bernard himself, had become the object of universal envy. The arrogation of the right of investiture by crosier and ring had been succeeded by violent usurpations and base and cowardly acts of simony.

"O vainglory!" cries Peter of Blois, "blind ambition I insatiable thirst for temporal honours! lust of office! ye are the worms that gnaw the heart and make shipwreck of the soul! Whence comes this plague, and whence this growing presumption, that urges the worthless to seek for office, and renders them the more desirous of obtaining, the less worthy they are to receive? Heedless of soul and body, these wretched ones lay hold on the pastoral office, an office fraught not only with danger to themselves but with perdition to all."[1] Thirty years previously, St. Bernard,

---

[1] *Lettre du Cardinal Octavien.*

with bitter irony, uttered these words:—"Schoolboys
and immature striplings are, on account of their lofty
birth, promoted to ecclesiastical dignities, and pass
from the discipline of the rod to the government of
the clergy; oftentimes more rejoiced at escape from
punishment, than flattered by filling a post of command; more delighted at their freedom from control,
than rejoiced at the dignity to which they have attained."[1] This is the woe of the Church; you behold
her, at the price of her own blood, converting infidel
nations, softening their manners and forming their
minds; clearing their forests and studding their
towns and their solitudes with houses of prayer;
then, after twenty generations of saints have enriched these tabernacles with every blessing of
heaven and of earth, instead of the rich man, whose
heart God had touched, coming to bewail his transgressions, and the poor man, so content with the will
of Heaven, that, bending his knees, he vowed to be
poorer still; instead of the saintly successors of the
saints, now there is to be seen but the poor man desiring riches, the rich man desiring power, and many
who even know not what they need.

Soon, by dint of intrigue, the episcopal and abba-
tial crosier falls into hands unhallowed by pure
intentions; the world has the delight of seeing its fa-
vourites ruling the Church of God and changing the
mild rule of Jesus Christ for that of secular power.
The cloisters re-echo to the yelping of hounds and the
neighing of steeds. Who now shall discern between

---

[1] *Lettre xlii. á Henri, Archevêque de Sens.*

the false vocation and the true? With whom will such skill be found? or who have leisure and thought to bestow on such a question as this? Earthly rank takes precedence of heavenly birth; and prayer, humility, penitence, and zeal, flee away like timid fledglings to their nests, and the tombs of the saints are forgotten even in the saints' own home.

Such was the sad condition to which a sacrilegious ambition had reduced a considerable number of the churches and monasteries in the West. The Holy See, although herself troubled by the schisms raised against her and fomented by the Emperor Frederic I., ceased not to provide remedies for these grave disorders. In fifty-six years three Œcumenical Councils had been called, but were unable to do more than partially carry out a reform which the illustrious successors of Gregory VII. were nevertheless privileged to effect.

One day, about the year 1160, Peter Valdo, a rich inhabitant of Lyons, saw one of his fellow-citizens fall at his side, struck by lightning. This accident led him to reflect: he distributed his goods among the poor and consecrated himself to the service of God. As the reform of the Church was then occupying all minds, his very zeal facilitated the belief that this was the mission to which he was called; and collecting around him a few individuals, he persuaded them to join him in embracing an apostolic life. How almost imperceptible is often the border-line between the thoughts that render man truly great and those that convert him into a mere disturber of the public peace! Had

Peter Valdo only possessed more virtue and more genius, he might have been a St. Dominic or a St. Francis of Assisi; but he gave way to a temptation to which, in all ages, many men of fairly lofty genius have succumbed. He did not believe it possible to save the Church by the Church, and declared that the true Spouse of Jesus Christ had, in the reign of Constantine, fallen away by her acceptance of temporal wealth; that the Church of Rome was the great harlot spoken of in the Apocalypse, the mother and mistress of all abominations; that the bishops were Scribes, the religious, Pharisees; that the Roman Pontiff and the whole of the episcopate were homicides; that the clergy ought to possess neither lands nor tithes; that it was sinful to endow churches or convents, and that all clerics should, after the example of the Apostles, work for their own living; in fine, that he, Peter Valdo, was about to re-establish, on its primitive foundations, the true Church of God, The whole force of the Waldensians lay in their direct attack on the Church, and in the real or apparent contrast of their manners with those of the clergy of their day. Arnold of Brescia, who was burnt at the stake in Rome, had been their precursor, a man whose figure stands forth on the page of history far more prominently than does that of Peter Valdo; but as the latter had the advantage of appearing on the scene later, and when the scandal had increased, his success was the more alarming. He was truly the Patriarch of Western heresies, and impressed them with one of the chief features distinguishing them from Greek heresies—to wit, a practical rather than metaphysical character.

Favoured by similar circumstances, a heresy of Oriental origin, already introduced into Germany and Italy, established its headquarters in the South of France. This heresy, always attacked, and never destroyed, dated from the end of the third century. It had sprung to life on the frontiers of Persia and the Roman Empire, and consisted of a blending of Christian with ancient Persian doctrines, attributing the mystery of the world to two conflicting principles, co-eternal with each other, the one good and the other evil. Such mixture of religious and philosophic ideas was then very general; the tendency of weak minds is to attempt to unite that which in reality is incompatible. A Persian named Manès gave the finishing touch to the monstrous alliance of which we speak. Less fortunate than other heresiarchs, his sect could never attain publicity, that is, have temples, priests, or any recognised followers. Imperial edicts, supported by public opinion, were perseveringly launched against it, and this prolonged its life. The state of public society is a proof that error can subsist but for a brief time, and this, shortened in proportion to the hollowness of its basis and the immorality of its teachings. Driven from the light of day, the Manicheans sought refuge in obscurity; they formed themselves into a secret society,—the only way this in which error can prolong its existence, the advantage of a secret association consisting less in the ease with which it enables them to elude the law, than the facility it affords them for escaping from the voice of public reason. Nothing can hinder a few

men, united by dogmas however perverse, and practices however ludicrous, from recruiting their
numbers out of the ranks of ill-balanced minds, from
attracting the romantic by the charm of initiatory
rites, from influencing them by means of dogmatic
precepts, retaining them by promise of a grand and
distant goal, the secret of which they imagine to have
been transmitted to themselves throughout a hundred preceding generations, and fascinating them by
the secrecy with which all is surrounded. Such a secret society exists at the present day, consisting of
perhaps no more than three initiates, and ascending
by an invisible chain even to the cave of Trophonius
or to the crypts of Egyptian temples. These men,
proud of their precious deposit, traverse the path of
ages, profoundly indifferent to all that is occurring,
judging of everything by the privileged doctrine
which has fallen to their lot, and pre-occupied with
the one desire of engendering a soul, to whom at their
own death they may transmit their precious legacy.
These are the *Jews* of error. Thus lived the Manicheans, appearing in history from time to time, like
those monsters who pursue their secret course in the
depths of the ocean, and whose gigantic form now
and again is seen above the surface. But their appearance in the twelfth century was rendered
striking by their assuming then, for the first time,
the form of a public society. Strange and unheard-of
spectacle! These sectaries, constantly kept in subjection by the Lower Empire, now openly established
themselves in France, beneath the eyes of those very
Pontiffs who were sufficiently powerful to compel

even the Emperor himself to respect the law of God and the will of Christian nations. Nothing reveals so clearly the reaction stealthily at work in Europe. Raymond VI., Count of Toulouse, was at the head of the French Manicheans, commonly called Albigenses. He was great-nephew to the celebrated Raymond, Count of St. Gilles, whose name is interwoven with the grandest names of the first Crusade, with those of such men as Godfrey of Bouillon, Baldwin, Robert, Hugh and Boëmond. Abandoning the heritage bequeathed to him by his ancestors, he headed the most detestable heresy to which the East had given birth, having himself succumbed to the secret mysteries of the Manicheans, and to the Waldensian disguise in which they had enveloped themselves, in order that they might the more easily gain access into the Western mind.

This was not all. The teaching of the Catholic School, now resumed after a long interval, became tinged with the hue of Aristotelian philosophy, the tendency of which was to give reason precedence of faith in the exposition of Christian dogmas. Abelard, a man more renowned for his faults than for his errors, had fallen victim to this mode of dealing with theology. St. Bernard accused him of changing faith, grounded on God's Word, into mere opinion, based on the principles and conclusions of human reason; and although St. Bernard gained an easy victory, and was honoured by the genuine submission and reconciliation of his adversary, the evil still continued. It is at all times difficult to withstand certain influences, proceeding from a remote and lofty centre; the

Grecian epoch was still held in high esteem by cultivated minds, and considered by them as the most
exalted point to which human genius could attain.
Christianity had not had leisure to create a literature
that would compare with that of Greece, nor form a
philosophy and science of her own. Doubtless, the
germ of such existed in the writings of the Fathers;
but, it being more convenient to accept a ready-made
form of philosophy and science, they accepted that of
Aristotle. Unfortunately, Aristotle and the Gospel do
not always agree; hence, three parties, one, sacrificing philosophy to Jesus Christ, according to these
words, *"Ye have but one Master, Christ;"* the other,
sacrificing Jesus Christ to philosophy, on the ground
that reason is the first light of man, and, as such,
must always retain its supremacy. The third party
admitted that there were two kinds of truth, that of
reason and that of faith, and that what was true in
the one might be false in the other.

In fine, heresy and schism, favoured by the corrupt state of ecclesiastical discipline and the revival
of pagan learning, threatened Christianity in the
West, at the same time that the non-success of the
Crusaders completed its ruin in the East, and opened
the gates of Christendom to the barbarians. True,
the Popes courageously resisted the increasing dan-
gers of the situation. They subdued the Emperor
Frederic I., animated the people to new crusades,
summoned councils for the suppression of error and
corruption, watched over the purity of doctrine in the
schools, and with a firm hand strengthened the alliance of European faith and thought; and from the

vigorous sap of this old pontifical tree Innocent III. sprang to life. No one individual can of himself sustain the weight of things human and divine; the greatest men need the reunion of a thousand concurrent forces, and those which Providence had granted to the past seemed insufficient for the future. The work of Clevis, St. Benedict, Charlemagne, and Gregory VII., still undestroyed, and animated by their genius, stood in need of a fresh effusion of that Spirit in whom alone is immortality. It is in such supreme moments as these that we must give heed to the counsels of God. Three hundred years later, He will abandon half Europe to error, in order one day to derive from that very error, triumphs, the secret of which we already begin to discern; but at that epoch it pleased Him to rescue His Church by the direct road of mercy. Jesus Christ glanced at His own hands and feet, wounded for our sakes, and from this look of love were born two men, St. Dominic and St. Francis of Assisi. The history of these two men, so similar, and yet so different, should never be separated, but that which God created in the same moment, no one pen can describe. It will be enough for us if we succeed in giving some faint idea of the holy Patriarch Dominic to those who have never studied his life.

CHAPTER II.

Parentage of St Dominic[1]

IN A VALLEY of Old Castile, watered by the Douro, and about equidistant from Aranda and Osma, stands a simple village, called in the language of the country Calarnéga, and Caleroga in the softer language of many historians. There was St. Dominic born, in the year 1170 of the Christian era. After God, he owed his existence to Felix de Gusman and Jeanne d'Aza. At Calarnéga this pious and noble pair possessed a residence, in which the Saint first saw the light, and part of which building is still in existence.

In 1266 Alphonso the Wise, king of Castile, in concert with his wife, sons, and leading grandees of Spain, founded a convent of Dominican nuns on the same spot. In this edifice are to be seen apartments of more ancient date, and differing in style from the rest of the building: a mediæval tower, bearing the arms of the Gusmans, a fountain named after them,

---

[1] At the end of this volume will be found a list of contemporary authors from whose writings I have derived the facts composing the Life of St. Dominic. I name them on the margin only when I quote them. For the verification of the rest see vol. i. of the *Annales de l'Ordre des Frères Prêcheurs*, by Father Mamachie. His work on St. Dominic, printed in Rome in 1756, is the most complete of any.

and many other vestiges, designated in the traditional language of the neighbourhood the *Palace of the Gusmans*. The chief seat of the Castilian branch of this noble house was a few miles distant; their place of sepulture, also near Calarnéga, was in the Cistercian church at Gumiel d'Izan. Thither were borne, after death, Felix de Gusman and Jeanne d'Aza, and they were interred in adjoining crypts. But the veneration in which they were held became ere long the cause of their separation. About the year 1318, John Emanuel, Infanta of Spain, caused the body of Jeanne d'Aza to be removed to the Dominican convent erected by him at Pennafied. Felix remained alone in his ancestral tomb, a faithful witness to the illustrious blood inherited by St. Dominic, and Jeanne rejoined the spiritual family of her son, that she might share in the glory he had acquired by preferring a heavenly to an earthly posterity.[1]

A wonderful sign heralded the birth of St. Dominic. His mother dreamt that she saw her child appear under the form of a dog, holding in its jaws a lighted torch, with which he kindled the whole world. Alarmed by this obscure presage, she frequently went to pray at the tomb of St. Dominic of Silos, formerly abbot of a monastery of the same name, not far from Calarnéga, and, in gratitude for the consolation vouchsafed her there, she bestowed the name of

---

[1] See a Latin treatise by Père Brémond, entitled, *De Gusmana Stirpe Sancti Dominici*, Romæ, 1740. The *completers* of Bollandu's *Acts of the Saints* expressed a doubt as to whether St. Dominic was descended from the Gusmans. Père Brémond has answered them in this work. The evidence with which it abounds sets the question at rest.

Dominic on the infant who had been the subject of so many prayers. He was the third child of this holy woman. The eldest, Antonio, dedicated his life to the service of the poor, and by his great charity adorned the priestly office to which he had been raised; the second, Mannès, died in the habit of the Order of Friar Preachers.

When Dominic was presented at the baptismal font, a new sign manifested his future greatness. His godmother, mentioned by historians merely as a lady of noble birth, beheld in a dream a radiant star on the brow of the newly baptized, the brilliancy of which seemed to remain on Dominic's countenance; and it was remarked, as a singular fact, that a constant radiancy illumined his brow, attracting the hearts of all beholders. The white marble font in which he had been baptized, was transported to the monastery of Friar Preachers at Valladolid in 1605, by command of Philip III., who desired that his son should be baptized therein. At the present day it is at St. Dominic's in Madrid, and many Spanish infants have there been initiated into the life that is in Christ Jesus our Lord.

No stranger's milk nourished St. Dominic; his mother would allow no blood but her own to circulate in his veins; at her breast he drank in his chaste nourishment, and from her lips he received the words of truth. In this maternal intercourse there was nought to fear, save the softness of his apparel, and those tender attentions which even the most Christian mother sometimes lavishes too freely on her child. But indwelling grace made him speedily revolt from any such yoke. As soon as he could move without assistance, he secretly left his cradle and took his rest upon the floor, as if he were already conscious of the misery of mankind, the difference of their lot here below, and was so moved with love for them that he could not endure that his couch should be better than theirs, or that, initiated in the secrets of Bethlehem, he desired a cradle like that of his Lord. We know nothing more of the first six years of his life.

Early in his seventh year he quitted the paternal roof, and was sent to his uncle, Gumiel d'Izan, archpresbyter of the church in that place. There, near the tomb of his ancestors, and under the twofold influence of authority and relationship, Dominic passed the second portion of his childhood. An historian remarks: "Ere the world had breathed on this child, he was intrusted, like Samuel, to the teaching of the Church, that he might benefit by her salutary discipline; and the result was, that, grounded on this firm foundation, he grew in stature and in wisdom, daily advancing in the paths of virtue." [1]

The University of Palencia, in the kingdom of Leon, the only one Spain then possessed, was the third school in which Dominic was trained. He went there at the age of fifteen, and for the first time in life found himself alone, far from the happy valley where, beneath the walls of Calarnéga and Gumiel d'Izan, he had bidden adieu to the happy memories of home.

He remained at Palencia ten years, of which he

---

[1] Constantin d'Orvieto, *Vie de S. Dominique*, ii. 3.

devoted the first six to the study of literature and
philosophy, as they were then taught. "But," says
another historian, "the angelic youth, although easily mastering all human science, was not enchanted
with it, because he found not there the Wisdom of
God, which is Christ. No philosopher has ever revealed this wisdom to man; none of the princes of this
world have known it; therefore, lest he should con-
sume the flower and strength of youth in fruitless
labours, and that he might quench his ardent thirst,
he turned to the deep wells of theology, invoking and
praying Christ, the Wisdom of the Father, that He
would open his heart to the true science, his ears to
the teaching of Holy Scripture. So sweet was this Divine Word to him, with such avidity and desire did
he receive it, that he passed his nights almost without sleep, giving to study the time he took from rest,
and that he might drink the more worthily and with
chaster lips from the fount of wisdom, he abstained
for nearly ten years from the use of wine. It was a
wondrous and pleasant sight to behold this man,
with the outward marks of extreme youth, but with
the mature conversation and strength of character
belonging to advanced years. Superior to the pleas-
ures of youth, he sought but for righteousness, and
anxious to lose no time in aimless studies, he turned
to his mother the Church, preferring the breasts of
her consolation and the repose of her tabernacles,
and passed his time in diligent work and prayer.

God rewarded him for the fervent love with which
he kept the commandments, by inspiring him with a
spirit of wisdom and intelligence which rendered the

most difficult questions easy for him to solve.[1]
Of his sojourn in Palencia two traits remain. During a famine that ravaged Spain, Dominic, not
content with giving to the poor all that he possessed,
even his very garments, sold the books annotated by
his own pen, so that he might give away the money
he received for them; and when surprise was manifested at his depriving himself of the means of study,
he uttered these words, the first that have been
handed down to us: "How can I study from dry parch-
ments when there are human beings dying of
hunger?" [2] Incited by his example, the University
professors and students generously came to the relief
of the unfortunate ones.   Another time, seeing a
woman, whose brother had been taken prisoner by
the Moors, weeping bitterly at her inability to provide his ransom, Dominic offered to sell himself in
order to redeem the captive; but God, having reserved him for the spiritual redemption of a great
multitude of human beings, did not permit him to
carry his purpose into effect.

When, at the close of autumn, the traveller passes
through a country cleared of all its harvests, he at
times meets with some fruit that has escaped the
hand of the labourer, and this remnant of past fertility suffices to enable him to judge of the unknown
tracts through which he has passed.   Thus Providence, while leaving in obscurity the youth of His

---

[1] Thierry d'Apolda, *Vie de St. Dominique*, ch. i. n. 17, 18.

[2] Actes de Bologne, deposition of Brother Stephen, n. 1.

servant Dominic, has nevertheless willed that history should preserve some traits, incomplete but
touching revelations of a soul where purity, grace, intelligence, truth, and every virtue was the effect of a
superabounding love to God and man. Dominic had
almost attained his twenty-fifth year without any
manifestation as yet of God's will concerning him. To
the man of the world life is but a short space, that he
traverses in the slowest possible manner and by the
most pleasant road. Not so does the Christian view
it; he knows that each man, as vicar of Jesus Christ,
must, by self-sacrifice, labour for the redemption of
the human race, and that in the plan of this grand
work each has his place assigned from eternity,—a
place which he is free to accept or refuse. He knows
that if he voluntarily desert the place Providence has
offered him in the ranks of useful beings, that place
will be given to a better than he, and he himself
abandoned to his own self-guidance along the broad,
short path of egotism. These thoughts occupy the
mind of the Christian who as yet knows not to what
he is predestined, and convinced that the surest way
of learning it is to desire to accomplish it whatever it
may be, he holds himself in readiness for all that God
may will. He despises none of the offices necessary
to the wellbeing of the Christian republic, because in
all may be found the three things on which their real
value depends—the will of God, who imposes them;
the good resulting from the faithful exercise of the
duties attendant thereon, and the fidelity of him to
whom they are intrusted. He believes firmly that the
least honoured are not necessarily the least noble,

and that the crown of the Saints never descends so swiftly from heaven as when destined to encircle the brow of the poor,—a brow grown hoary in lowly and humble service. Little cares he where God shall mark his place; it is sufficient for him to know what is the will of God. God had prepared for young Dominic an intermediary worthy of Himself, who would not only reveal to him his vocation, but open to him the gates of his future career, conducting him by unforeseen paths to the place of action where Providence was awaiting him.

Among the means of reform had recourse to by such as desired the re-establishment of ecclesiastical discipline was one specially recommended by the Sovereign Pontiff, to wit, the introduction of community life among the clergy. Thus had the Apostles lived; and St. Augustine, their copyist, has bequeathed to us the famous Rule that bears his name. Community life is neither more nor less than family life carried to its highest degree of perfection, and it is impossible for it to be faithfully practised without those who have devoted themselves to it being inspired with those sentiments of fraternity, poverty, patience, and abnegation, in which the very soul of Christianity consists.

For about a century and a half they gave the name of canons-regular to priests leading this kind of life. They did not form one body under one head, but each house had its own prior, amenable only to the bishop. The one exception is the Order of Canons-Regular of Prémontré, founded by St. Norbert in 1120. Now, the

Bishop of Osma, Martin of Bazan, desirous of contributing to the restoration of discipline in the Church, had recently converted the canons of his cathedral into canons-regular, and learning that there was at the University of Palencia a young man of rare merit belonging to his diocese, he conceived the hope of attaching him to his chapter and interesting him in his plans of reform. He intrusted the negotiation of this matter to the person who had been his chief support in the arduous work he had just accomplished, a man illustrious by birth, genius, learning, and the venerable beauty of his life, and who later on united to these qualities, not peculiar to himself alone, a title that none can dispute. For six centuries the Spaniard Don Diégo de Azévédo has reposed in a tomb which I have not even seen, and yet I never utter his name but with profound respect, for he was the intermediary chosen by God to enlighten and guide the Patriarch of a dynasty of which I am the child; and when I trace back the long chain of my spiritual ancestors, I behold him as the connecting link between St. Dominic and Christ.

History has preserved no record of the early conversations between Don Diégo and the youthful Gusman, but the result makes it easy to divine them. At twenty-five a generous soul seeks but to sacrifice itself, and, full of love and vigour, only demands of Heaven and earth a noble cause to serve. And if this be true of a soul indebted for its character to nature alone, how much more is it true of him in whose soul Christianity and natural disposition blend together as two pure streams, not one drop of whose waters

has been lavished on vain passions! It is easy for me
to picture Don Diégo and the noble student of Palencia. He learnt in few words what no book, no
university, could teach: the existing struggle between good and evil in the world; the deep wounds
inflicted on the Church; the general tendency of
things; and, in fine, all that constituted the inner secret of the age. Initiated into the evils of the time, by
a man who understood them, Dominic doubtless felt
the necessity of devoting himself soul and body to the
cause of suffering Christendom. He saw at a glance
his place and his work—saw them to be in the ranks
of that priesthood according to Melchisedec; that he
was to follow the steps of Jesus Christ, sole Saviour
of the world, sole Source of all truth, goodness, grace,
peace, self-devotion, and whose enemies, take what
name they may, are the eternal foes of the human
race. He saw that this divine priesthood, defiled by
many, unworthy of their consecration, needed to be
re-exalted in the sight of God and man; and that this
could only be effected by a revival of apostolic virtues
in those who had been admitted to and honoured
with the priestly office. And as the first step in all
reforms is to be oneself what one wishes others to be,
the heir of the Gusmans dedicated his life to God in
the reformed chapter of Osma, under the direction of
Don Diégo, prior at that time.

"Then," says the Blessed Jourdain of Saxony, "he
appeared among, his brethren, the canons, as a shin-
ing light, foremost in sanctity, but in his own esteem
lowest of all, shedding around him a life-giving
odour, and a perfume, sweet as incense in summer-

time. His brethren, admiring so lofty a piety, elected him sub-prior, in order that his exaltation might render his example more visible and more potent. He, like a flourishing olive-tree and growing cypress, remained day and night in the church, applying himself constantly to prayer, and scarcely ever quitting the cloister for fear of shortening his time for contemplation. God had given him a deep sorrow for sinners, for the afflicted and the miserable, whose woes Dominic enshrined in his inner sanctuary of compassion, and the deep loving sorrow he felt for them was so intense as to seek relief in tears. His almost constant habit was to pass the night in prayer and communion with God; and so great at times was his emotion, that from his closed chamber audible proofs of the same often proceeded. One thing he asked often and earnestly from God; it was that He would bestow on him a true charity, a love that would render it easy to give up all for the salvation of men, convinced that only then would he be a true member of Christ when he should consecrate himself with all his powers to win souls, after the example of the Saviour of the world, the Lord Jesus Christ, who gave Himself for our redemption. He was reading a book entitled *Conferences of the Fathers*, treating of vice and spiritual perfection, and in perusing it he strove to know and follow all the paths of righteousness. By God's grace this book enabled him to attain to an unusual degree of purity of conscience, abundant light in meditation, and a very great perfection." [1]

---

[1] *Vie de St. Dominique*, ch. i. n. 8, &c.

Though Dominic's life was to be but short, Providence was in no hurry, and allowed him to spend nine years at Osma in order to fit himself for the as yet unknown mission which he was destined to fulfil. In this interval, in the year 1201, Don Diégo de Azévédo succeeded Martin de Bazan in the episcopal see. Almost at the same time Dominic began his public preaching, but without going far from Osma; and probably continued this ministry, regarding which we have no particulars, until 1203, the solemn moment when, at the age of twenty-four, he quitted Spain and went forth all unconsciously to meet his destiny.

Here ends the training of St. Dominic, that is to say, the chain of events by which his mind and soul were fashioned, and which prepared him for the end which Providence intended him to accomplish. Each man has a particular training, suited to his future work in the world, the knowledge of which is requisite to the full understanding of his character. Friendship opens up to us those deep recesses where the mysteries of the past and future are concealed; confession also reveals the same, but in another intent; history too makes her search there, in order to seize events at their fountain-head and trace back their clue to Him who created the germ and enriched it with its countless forms of good. Called by God to be founder of a new Order that should edify the world by poverty, preaching, and heavenly wisdom, Dominic's training was in conformity with this predestination. He is born of a noble family, because

voluntary poverty is the more striking in one who re-
nounces the rank and riches which are his by birth.
He is born in Spain, far from the land which should
be the scene of his apostolate, because one of the
greatest sacrifices to an apostle is the quitting his
native land in order to enlighten nations whose very
language is unknown to him. The first ten years of
his youth are spent at the University, that he may
acquire the learning necessary for the evangelical office, and transmit it to, and cause it to be held in high
esteem by, his Order. During the following nine
years he conforms to the observances of community
life, so that by thoroughly understanding its difficulties and its virtues, he may at a future day impose on
his brethren no yoke but such as he himself had long
borne. Front his very cradle God endows him with
an instinctive love of rigorous self-denial; for how
shall the Apostle endure the fatigue of long journeys,
heat, cold, hunger, imprisonment, blows, and misery,
unless he early subjects his body to the rudest trials?
God also gives him an early and ardent love of
prayer; for prayer is the omnipotent act which places
Heaven's might at man's disposal. Heaven is inac-
cessible to violence; prayer brings Heaven down to
us. But, over and above all, Dominic receives the gift
without which all other gifts are nought—the gift of
charity, so great that it impels him day and night to
devote himself to the salvation of his brethren, whose
afflictions move him even to tears. In fine, God sends
him a man of marked strength of character, who becomes his friend and his bishop, and who, as we shall
ere long see, will introduce him to France and to

Rome. These few connected and important facts form a circle of thirty-four years, and, moulded by their influence, Dominic attains, unblemished, the most perfect form of manhood to which the God-fearing man can aspire.

CHAPTER III.

*St. Dominic arrives in France.—His First Journey to
Rome.—Interview at Montpellier.*

A T THAT TIME, Alphonso III., king of Castile, was
meditating a marriage between his son and a
Danish princess, and intrusted the negotiation of the
affair to the Bishop of Osma, who, taking with him
Dominic, set out for the North of Germany towards
the close of the year 1203. In passing through
Languedoc, both were deeply grieved at beholding
the alarming success of the Albigenses. On reaching
Toulouse, where they had to pass the night, Dominic
perceived that their host was a heretic; and although
time pressed, he was anxious to be of service to the
poor deluded man under whose roof they then were.
Jesus Christ has said to His Apostles, *"When you
come into a house, salute it, saying, Peace be to this
house. And if that house be worthy, your peace shall
come upon it; but if it be not worthy, your peace shall
return to you."* [1] The Saints, to whose minds all the
words of Jesus Christ are ever present, and who
know the power of a benediction given even in secret,
regard themselves as God's ambassadors to every
creature whom they meet, and strive to part from

---

[1] St. Matthew x. 12, 13.

none until they have implanted in his heart some germ of grace. Dominic did not rest content with merely praying for his host, but passed the night in converse with him; and the ready eloquence of the stranger made so deep an impression on the heretic, that he returned to the faith before the dawn of day.

Then another wonder occurred; touched by the conquest he had just effected in the cause of truth, and also by the sad spectacle of the ravages made by false doctrine, Dominic then first conceived the idea of founding an Order in defence of the Church, the mission of which should consist in preaching. This sudden resolve took lasting possession of his mind; and now that the secret of his future career was revealed to him, he quitted France, as if that land, jealous that this great man owed her not his birth, had nevertheless obtained from God this favour, that he should not tread her soil in vain, and that to her he should be indebted for the decisive counsel of his life.

After much fatigue, Don Diégo and Dominic reached their journey's end; and finding the Danish Court favourably disposed to the alliance desired by Castile, they at once returned with these tidings to King Alphonso, and again set forth with larger retinue to escort the Princess to Spain; but she died during the interim, and Don Diégo, finding himself relieved of his mission, sent a courier to the king, and turned his own steps to Rome.

At that time there was no Christian but desired, ere death, to press with his lips the shrines of the holy Apostles Peter and Paul. Even the poor came on foot to visit these distant relics, and receive, at least once, the blessing of the Vicar of Jesus Christ.

Don Diégo and Dominic knelt side by side at that tomb which governs the world; and as they raised their foreheads from the dust, a second happiness awaited them—a happiness exceeding all other that a Christian can experience on earth—that of beholding the Pontifical See filled by a worthy occupant. Such was Innocent III. What were the feelings awakened in them by sight of the Universal City, history does not record. They who come to Rome for the first time, bearing with them the grace of Christianity and the charm of youth, know the emotion that Rome awakes; others would not comprehend it so readily; and I admire the sobriety of those old historians who, when they knew the impotence of language, wisely kept silence.

The Bishop of Osma intended to ask a favour of the Sovereign Pontiff. He had determined to resign his see and consecrate the remainder of his days to evangelising the Cumans, a barbarous people dwelling on the confines of Hungary, and renowned for their cruelty. Innocent III. refusing to accede to this heroic demand, Don Diégo entreated that he might, while still retaining his bishopric, be permitted to go on his missionary work; but the Pope persisted in his refusal, and commanded him to return to his diocese. The two pilgrims re-crossed the Alps in the spring of 1205, and although intending to proceed at once to Spain, they gratified their pious wish of visiting on their way one of the most renowned monasteries of Christendom; and taking a long and circuitous route, knocked for admittance at the gate of the Abbey of Cîteaux.

The spirit of St. Bernard still dwelt there; and if the same poverty no longer reigned, there were other virtues, which so won the heart of the Bishop that he expressed to the monks his wish to receive their habit. This request was at once complied with, and the monastic garb in some degree consoled him for being unable to go forth as a poor missionary to the Cumans. Although Dominic refrained from following his friend's example, he carried away feelings of deep esteem and affection for the monks of Cîteaux. After a short sojourn at the abbey, they both resumed their journey; and following, most probably, the banks of the Saone and the Rhone, arrived at Montpellier.

Three men who played an important part in the affairs of the Church at that epoch were then assembled beneath the walls of Montpellier. Arnault, abbot of Cîteaux; Raoul and Pierre de Castelnau, monks of the same Order. Pope Innocent III. had appointed them Legates Apostolic to the provinces of Aix, Aries, and Narbonne, with full powers to follow the course they judged best for the repression of heresy. Their legateship, of more than a year's duration, had hitherto been unsuccessful. The Count of Toulouse, governor of those provinces, openly supported the heretics; the bishops refused to aid the Legates, one from cowardice, another from indifference, and a third because he was a heretic too. "The clergy had incurred the contempt of the people to such a degree," says Guillaume de Puy-Laurens, "that the name of ecclesiastic had passed into a proverb like that of Jew, so that instead of saying, 'I would rather be a Jew than do that,' many would substitute the word 'ecclesiastic.' On appearing in public, they would carefully brush their hair so as to conceal their tonsure, which they made as small as possible. The Knights very rarely destined their own sons for the ecclesiastical state, but presented the sons of their retainers to those churches of which they received the tithes, and the Bishops conferred orders on whom they could."[1] Innocent III. had not concealed from his Legates the extent of this evil; in a letter dated May 31, 1204, he said, "Those called by St. Peter to share his charge over Israel do not keep watch over the flock by night, but sleep, and come not to the rescue of Israel from the hands of the Midianites. The shepherd is become a hireling; he feeds not the flock, but himself; he seizes the wool and the milk of the sheep; abandons the fold to the ravages of the wolf, and offers no resistance to the foes of the house of God. Hireling as he is, he flees from the evil that he could destroy, and treacherously becomes its protector. The majority have deserted the cause of God, and of the remainder, few render Him any service."[2]

The three Legates were men of strong faith and noble character, but, abandoned by all, were unable to effect anything either by authority or persuasion. In those provinces not a single bishop would support them in exhorting Count Raymond VI. to remember

---

[1] *Chronicle*, in the prologue.
[2] *Letters* of Innocent III., book vii. letter 75.

the glorious conduct of his ancestors. Their conferences had been unsuccessful with the heretics, who
always cited the deplorable lives of the clergy, quot-
ing our Lord's own words, "By their fruits ye shall
know them"[1] In spite of their energetic character,
the Legates became dejected, and bitterly felt how
impossible it is to withstand, unaided, the torrent of
human passions when directed against the truth;
and under the weight of this conviction they were deliberating at Montpellier. Their unanimous decision
was to give the Sovereign Pontiff an exact account of
the state of things, at the same time resigning into
his hands an office, the duties of which they could
fulfil neither with honour nor profit. But *man's necessity is God's opportunity.*

During the last thirty years Providence had been
preparing an answer to the cries of His servants and
the insults of His enemies, and now the hour for deliverance had come. At the very moment that the
Legates were making their sorrowful resolutions,
they learnt that Don Diégo, Bishop of Osma, had just
arrived at Montpellier. They sent a message entreating him to come and see them: Don Diégo at once
acceded.

I shall allow the Blessed Jourdain de Saxe to continue the narrative: "The Legates received him with
respect, and begged his advice, knowing that he was
a holy man, and full of zeal for the faith. He, endowed as he was with the gift of circumspection and

---

[1] St. Matthew vii. 16.

skilled in the ways of God, began to inquire concerning the manners and customs of the heretics. He observed that they made converts by their persuasive manners, by preaching, and by an exterior of sanctity, while the Legates were surrounded by a numerous and stately retinue. He replied, 'My brothers, you must change your course of action. It seems to me impossible to convert, by words, men who set such store by example; they seduce simple souls by the outward appearances of evangelical poverty and austerity, and while you present the contrary spectacles you will edify but little; you will do much harm, and you will never touch their heart. Oppose example to example: to feigned sanctity oppose true piety: it is only by a marked humility that one gains the victory over the feigned sanctity of false apostles. Thus it was that St. Paul's boasting opponents obliged him to remind them of his own virtues, austerities, and the continual perils to which his life was exposed.' The Legates rejoined, 'Most excellent father, what do you advise us to do?' He replied, 'Do as I do;' and at once, filled with the Spirit of God, he called his attendants and ordered them to return to Osma with his equipages and sumptuous retinue. He only retained a few ecclesiastics, and declared his intention of remaining in those parts to render service to the faith. He also retained near his person the Superior Dominic, whom he highly esteemed and loved; this was Brother Dominic, founder of the Order of Preachers, and who from that moment called himself no longer sub-prior, but Brother Dominic; truly a man of God, as his purity of life and zeal for the commandments testify. The Legates, moved by the counsel and example they had received, at once consented; dismissed their baggage and attendants, and keeping only such books as were necessary for controversy, went on foot in a state of voluntary poverty, and under the guidance of the Bishop of Osma, to preach the true faith."[1]

How marvellously and patiently God brought about this issue! On the shores of a river in Spain, two men, differing in age, receive an abundant outpouring of the Spirit of God. One day they meet, attracted by the odour of their mutual virtues, like two rare trees planted in the same forest, whose branches bend to meet each other. Then, when a lengthened friendship has blended their thoughts and days in one, an unforeseen will summons them from their native land, leads them through Europe, from the Pyrenees to the Baltic, from the Tiber to the hills of Burgundy, and, unconsciously to themselves, they arrive at the exact moment to give to three men, whose courage had almost failed, a counsel that changes the face of affairs, saves the honour of the Church, and prepares for her, in the near future, a legion of apostles! The enemies of the Church have never read her history attentively, or they would have remarked the inexhaustible fertility of her resources, and the marvellous adaptability of the same. She resembles that giant, sprung from the earth, who from his very fall received fresh strength; misfortune does but restore her pristine virtues, and in

---

[1] *Vie de St. Dominique*, ch. i. n. 16, &c.

losing the power lent her by the world, she but recovers her own native power. The world can only deprive her of that which it has bestowed, namely, participation in the benefits arising from riches, rank, secular honours and protection; vestments these, woven by impure hands, which, as the tunic of Dejanira, the Church must never wear save above the sackcloth of her native poverty. If gold, in lieu of being the handmaid of charity and the ornament of virtue, prove detrimental to the one or the other, then must gold perish, and the world, in spoiling the Church, does but restore to her the nuptial robe, the gift of her Divine Spouse, of which none can deprive her. For how rob her who possesses nought, or how spoil her whose treasure poverty is? It is in voluntary renunciation that God has made the strength of His Church consist, and no mortal hand can rob her of that treasure. This is why crafty persecutors have sought less to despoil, than corrupt the Church; most subtle form of evil this; and all would be lost by this ruse, if God permitted the evil to be universal. But from corruption springs forth life, and from her very ruins conscience awakes to vitality. Mystic circle, of which God holds the secret, and by which He governs all.

What could appear more hopeless than the religious condition of Languedoc in the year 1205? The Prince a violent heretic; the majority of the Barons favouring heresy; the Bishops utterly negligent of their duties; and some of them, as the Bishop of Toulouse and the Archbishop of Auch, stained with open crime; the clergy fallen in public esteem; but a small number of faithful Catholics left; the Church insulted by the specious show of virtue assumed by heresy; and even those were dispirited in whose strong pure hearts unshaken faith had its home. Two passing strangers suffice to change all. They will revive the courage of the Apostolic Legates, confirm the wavering, console the strong souls, rouse the Episcopate from its lethargy; a great Bishop will rule the See of Toulouse; and if success is not decisive, it will nevertheless be sufficiently marked to show on what side are reason, sound judgment, devotedness, and the assurance of a divine cause.

CHAPTER IV.

Apostolate of St. Dominic, from the interview at Montpellier to the commencement of the Albigensian War.—Founding of the Monastery of Notre-Dame-de-Prouille.

T HAT which the Apostolic Legates and the Bishop of Osma had decided on was at once carried into effect. The Abbot of Cîteaux left for Burgundy, in order to preside in the general chapter of his Order, promising to bring back with him a certain number of evangelical labourers. The two other Legates, Don Diégo, Dominic, and a few Spanish priests, set out on foot for Narbonne and Toulouse, stopping in the towns and villages on their route, as the Spirit of God moved them, or as external circumstances made them judge their preaching would be of use. When they had decided on evangelising any spot, they proportioned their stay either to the importance of the place or the impression that they made. In the churches they preached to the Catholics, and in private houses held their controversies with the heretics. Such conferences are of very remote antiquity. St. Paul frequently held such with the Jews, St. Augustine with the Donatists and African Manicheans. If perversity of will be one cause of error, ignorance is perhaps a more general one. The majority of men oppose truth through ignorance of the truth, and because they represent it to themselves under a false exterior. Therefore one of the duties of the apostolate consists in clearly setting forth the true faith, freed from the mists with which error and ignorance have obscured her, at the same time leaving to the human intellect all the liberty which the Word of God, and its interpreter, the Church, allow. But this exposition is serviceable, only so far as it attracts those who stand in need of it, and complete, only when both sides have equal freedom of discussion. This is the aim of all controversies in which honest men challenge honest men to enter the lists, and where speech is a weapon at the service of all, and conscience, the only judge. Although these controversies were in themselves nothing new, they were marked by a novel and daring feature. The Catholics often chose their adversaries as umpires, referring matters to their decision. They requested some of the leading heretics to preside in the meeting, declaring beforehand that they would accept their decision regarding the weight of the arguments brought forward on either side. Such heroic confidence was crowned with success, and they often had the satisfaction not only of knowing that they had not presumed too much on the human heart, but they also received a striking proof of the sources of good that lie hidden there.

Caraman, near Toulouse, was one of the first towns where they made any stay; and they preached with such success during a whole week, that the inhabitants granted to drive away the heretics, and, when our missionaries set forth, they escorted them some distance on their way. They remained a fortnight at Béziers, where their little army experienced a diminution of its ranks by the withdrawal of the Legate, Pierre de Castelnau, whom his friends persuaded to depart, on account of the great hatred which the heretics evinced for him. A third station was held at Carcassonne; another at Verfeil, in the vicinity of Toulouse; another at Fanjeaux, a small town situated on an eminence between Carcassonne and Pamiers, and which spot is rendered celebrated by the miraculous occurrence that took place there, and which the Blessed Jourdain de Saxe thus relates:—"An important conference was held at Fanjeaux in presence of a great number of the faithful and of the heretics. The Catholics had drawn up several outlines of arguments and authorities in support of the faith, but on comparing them, they gave the preference to those of God's blessed servant Dominic, and resolved to make use of his production in answer to the document put forth by the heretics. Three umpires were unanimously elected to decide on which side lay the most powerful arguments and consequently the soundest faith. Now, after much discussion, these umpires, finding themselves unable to come to any decision, suddenly resolved to throw the writings into the fire, so that if one escaped the flames they would know that it contained the true doctrine. The fire was kindled, the two volumes were thrown in; that of the heretics was consumed immediately, and the other, written by Dominic, the blessed servant of God, not only remained intact, but was cast out by the flames, and that in presence of the whole assembly. Twice, and thrice they returned it to the flames, and each time the result clearly manifested on which side lay the true faith and what was the sanctity of the writer."[1]

The remembrance of this prodigy lived not only on the page of history, but in the memory of the people of Fanjeaux, who in the year 1325 obtained from the king, Charles le Bel, permission to purchase the house where the event occurred, and to erect a sanctuary there, which the Sovereign Pontiffs have enriched with many privileges. A similar miracle took place at Montreal, but secretly, among the heretics, who had met during the night in order to examine another of the writings of this servant of God. They had agreed among themselves to conceal this prodigy; but one of them becoming converted, made the secret known.

Meanwhile Dominic had remarked, that one cause of the progress of heresy was the address with which the heretics took in their own hands the education of the daughters of those noble families who were too poor to give them an education suitable to their rank. He meditated how he might, with God's help, find a remedy for this, and thought the best plan would be to found a convent, in which to shelter those young Catholics whose birth and whose poverty exposed them to the snares of heresy. At the village of

---

[1] *Vie de St. Dominique*, ch. i. n. 20.

Prouille, situated in a plain at the foot of the Pyrenees, between Fanjeaux and Montreal, was a church
dedicated to the Blessed Virgin, and long held in
great veneration by the people. Dominic was much
attached to this church, and had often offered up his
prayers there whilst on his missionary journeys. On
crossing the Pyrenees to enter Languedoc, the humble sanctuary of Notre-Dame-de-Prouille dawned on
his vision as a sanctuary of hope and consolation, and
on that spot, close to the church, he erected his monastery, with the full consent and support of the
Bishop Foulques, recently appointed to the See of
Toulouse. Foulques was a Cistercian monk, eminent
for the purity of his life and the ardour of his faith,
and elected by the Catholics of Toulouse as their
Bishop, in place of Raymond de Rabenstens, whom a
pontifical decree had deprived of the episcopate. The
elevation of Foulques to so important a See caused
universal joy in the Church, and when the Legate
Pierre de Castelnau heard of the event, though then
dangerously ill, he rose from his bed, and with up-
lifted hands rendered thanks to Heaven. The Bishop
took Dominic and Don Diégo at once into his friendship, furthered with all his might the erection of the
convent, to which he granted first the use, and later
on the possession, of the church of Sainte-Marie, at
the side of which St. Dominic had built his monastery. Bérenger, Archbishop of Narbonne, had
already preceded him in this generous course by giving to the nuns, four months after their enclosure,
the church of St. Martin de Limoux, and all the revenues appertaining to the same. In the course of

time, Count Simon of Montfort and other Catholics
of distinction bestowed large benefactions on
Prouille, which soon became a flourishing and celebrated convent. One signal grace seemed always
vouchsafed to it: The civil and religious war, which
broke out soon after, respected its walls, and whilst
churches were ravaged, monasteries destroyed, and
armed heresy was often victorious, poor defenceless
women prayed in security within the walls of their
newly erected cloister; and the reason was this: The
early works of the Saints have a virgin purity which
moves the heart of God, and He who shields the tender blade from the fury of the tempest, keeps guard
over the cradle of momentous events.

What were the rules and habits of the sisters of
Prouille at that early date, we cannot with certainty
say. They had a prioress, but she was under the authority of Dominic, who retained the administration
both of the spiritual and temporal affairs of the convent, so that he might include his dear daughters in
his future Order, of which they were the first beginning. But as his apostolic labours prevented his
residing at Prouille, he intrusted the administration
of its temporal affairs to an inhabitant of Pamiers
who was much attached to Dominic, and whose name
was Guillaume Claret. The spiritual administration
was shared by Dominic with one or two French or
Spanish ecclesiastics, whose names are not known.
Part of the convent, outside the enclosure, contained
the apartments of Dominic and of his coadjutors, so
that this dwelling, distinct and yet under the same
roof, might be a guarantee of the unity which would

one day subsist between the Friar Preachers and the Dominicanesses, two branches springing from the same trunk. On the 27th December 1206, Feast of St. John the Evangelist, all preparations being completed, Dominic had the happiness of throwing open the gates of Notre-Dame-de-Prouille to many noble ladies desirous of consecrating themselves to God, under his direction.

As the first recipient of the world's redemption was a poor virgin daughter of David, so the earliest of the Dominican institutions was an asylum to protect the triple helplessness of sex, rank, and poverty. In its solitude and simplicity, at the foot of the Pyrenees, Notre-Dame-de-Prouille waited long and patiently the countless numbers of religious who should one day be her portion, and bear her name even to the very ends of the world. Eldest daughter of a father, himself slowly moulded by the patient training of God, she grew up in silence, honoured by the friendship and protection of many noble men. Dominic, who since the interview at Montpellier had renounced the title of Sub-Prior of Osma, now added to the lowly name of Brother Dominic that of Prior of Prouille. Some time after, having preached at Fanjeaux, Dominic, according to his usual custom, was praying in the church, when nine noble ladies prostrated themselves at his feet, exclaiming, "Servant of God, help us. If what you have preached to-day be true, our minds have been long blinded by error; for until now we have believed and followed with all our hearts those whom you call heretics, and we call *good men*. Now we know not what to think. Servant of

God, have pity on us, and pray the Lord your God to reveal to us the true faith." Dominic, having passed a few moments in silent prayer, replied, "Have patience, and fear nothing. I believe that God, who wills the death of none, will show you what master you have served till now." Then they suddenly beheld the spirit of error and hatred, under the form of an unclean animal, and Dominic, reassuring them, said, "From what God has just shown you, you may easily know what master you have served in following the heretics." [1] Then these women, rendering thanks to God, became firm converts to the Catholic faith, and many of them consecrated themselves to God in the convent of Prouille.

The Albigenses and the Catholics held a conference at Montreal in the year 1207. The Catholics selected from among their opponents four umpires, to whom both parties intrusted their writings on the disputed points. The public discussion lasted a fortnight, at the end of which period the umpires retired without giving any decision. Their conscience convinced them that the Catholics were in the right, but they had not the courage to give a decision adverse to their own party; and yet, notwithstanding this, a hundred and fifty men abjured heresy and returned to the bosom of the Church. The Legate, Pierre de Castelnau, was present at this conference, and soon after there arrived at Montreal the Abbot of Cîteaux, twelve other Abbots of the same Order, and about

---

[1] Le B. Humbert, *Vie de St. Dominique*, n. 44.

twenty Religious, all men of courage, learned in divine things, and whose holiness of life was worthy of
the mission they came to fulfil. They left Cîteaux at
the close of the general chapter, and set forth on their
journey, taking with them, in accordance with the
Bishop of Osma's advice, nothing save what was absolutely necessary. This reinforcement gave new
vigour to the Catholics, who, after two trying years,
at last beheld the fruit of their labours, experiencing
the truth of the promise that God will not forsake
those who work for Him in sincerity and truth. The
province of Narbonne had been evangelised throughout; conversions had been effected; the pride of the
heretics had been humbled by the sight of virtues of
which they themselves were incapable; and those
who carefully watched the movement that was going
on, knew that the Church was still alive. Under
Foulques the episcopate revived. Navarre, Bishop of
Concerans, followed his example, the weak among
their colleagues awoke from their lethargy, and the
poor Catholic nobles were encouraged by the erection
of the convent at Prouille. The grandest result was
the having united in one common thought (that of the
apostolate) so many men eminent for their virtue,
learning, and reputation, and the having given to
this rising apostolate an unhoped-for character of
stability. Nevertheless, unity was wanting to these
elements, then under the control of four different authorities, the Legates, Bishops, Cistercian Abbots,
and Spaniards. The necessity of establishing a Religious Order, the peculiar office of which should

consist in preaching, had often been a subject of discussion; and the arrival of the Cistercians at Montreal not only strengthened them in this conviction, but also inspired them with the desire of proceeding still further. The Bishop of Osma, though in rank inferior to the Legates, and, as a foreign Bishop, not independent of the French Prelates, was in reality the head of this movement. He came to the rescue when all seemed lost; was the first to put his hand to the work, without one backward glance; and had even won the affections of the heretics, so that they had declared "it was impossible but that such a man was predestined to salvation, and that doubtless he had only been sent in their midst to learn the true faith."[1] That hidden power which assigns each man his post, had given him precedence of the rest. He determined to return to Spain in order to settle the affairs of his diocese, collect funds for the convent of Prouille, which stood in need of help, bring back fresh labourers with him to France, in order to profit by the existing state of things, and having formed this resolution, started on foot for Spain.

On entering Pamiers, Don Diégo found the Bishops of Toulouse and Concerans, and a number of Abbots from different monasteries, who, having heard of his arrival, had come to do him honour. Their presence gave rise to a celebrated dispute with the Vaudois, who flourished in Pamiers under the protection of the Count of Foix. The Count invited the heretics and Catholics, by turns, to dine with

[1] Le B. Jourdain de Saxe, *Vie de St. Dominique*, ch. i. n. 1.

him, and offered his palace for them to hold their conference in. The Catholics chose one of their most
violent adversaries, belonging to the leading aristoc-
racy of the town, as umpire. The result far exceeded
all expectation. The umpire, Arnauld de Campran-
ham, pronounced in favour of the Catholics, and
abjured heresy. Another heretic of note, Durand de
Huesca, not only became a Catholic, but embraced
the religious life in Catalonia, whither he had retired, and became the founder of a new Congregation
known by the name of *Poor Catholics.* These two ab-
jurations—there   were   others   also—created   a
profound sensation in the town of Pamiers, and the
Catholics received many proofs of the joy and esteem
of the people. After this triumph, by which his apostolate was so worthily crowned, Don Diégo took leave
of those who had met to do him honour on his departure from France. Whether Dominic accompanied
him so far, we know not; it may be that their parting
took place at Prouille, and that beneath its much-
loved roof they beheld each other for the last time,
for God, in His impenetrable counsels, had decreed
that they should meet no more on earth.

Don Diégo traversed the Pyrenees and Aragon,
still on foot, revisited Osma, sat once more on his
episcopal throne—from which he had been absent
three years—and just as he was about to leave his
native land again, God called him to the heavenly
abode of angels and of men. His body was interred
in one of the churches at Osma, with this brief inscription: *"Here lies Diégo de Azévédo, Bishop of*

Osma; he died in the year 1245."[1] His death, announced so simply to posterity, nevertheless
produced an effect which clearly manifested the
greatness of the man. Hardly had the report of his
death crossed the Pyrenees, when the heroic work set
on foot by him suddenly collapsed. The abbots and
monks of Cîteaux went back to their monasteries; the
majority of the Spaniards left by Don Diégo under
Dominic's direction, returned to Spain. Of the three
Legates, Raoul had just died, Arnault disappeared
almost immediately, and Pierre de Castelnau was in
Provence, on the eve of falling victim to the blows of
an assassin. There remained but one man mindful
of Toulouse and Montpellier—a man who, still
young, and a foreigner, with no jurisdiction, and who
had not even appeared in the foremost ranks, could
not all at once replace such a man as Azévédo, whose
genius and piety were enhanced by his episcopal office, by his age, and by his celebrity. Dominic could
do no more than resist succumbing to this heavy be-
reavement and remain steadfast under the loss of
such a friend. Eight laborious years were requisite
to repair the void, and never did man at first gravi-
tate more slowly to, and then attain with such
marvellous rapidity, the end he had in view.

Miracles were wrought at the tomb of Azévédo,
and later on a chapel was erected to St. Dominic, in
the same edifice, where, beneath the effigy of the one,
pious hands laid the other to rest; but, as if Dominic

---

[1] The Spanish era began thirty-eight years before the Christian era.

would not permit that he who had been his guide on earth should remain in such a lowly position, reverent hands transferred the head of Don Diégo to the monastery of the Friar Preachers at Malaga. In spite of these marks of respect, adequate justice has not been done to his memory. France had but a passing glimpse of him; Spain saw him only for a short time; ere his work was consummated, death summoned him away. Destined by God to be only the forerunner of one more holy and more extraordinary than himself—no easy task this, and one which presupposes a perfectly unselfish heart—Azévédo fulfilled this task with the same simplicity that prompted him to cross the Pyrenees on foot. He never thought of self; but the posterity of Dominic evinces for him an esteem proportioned to the greatness of his humility, and I take my leave of him with the emotion of a son who has just closed the eyes of a departed father.

The death of the Bishop of Osma threw everything into confusion. Dominic stood almost alone; and as the two or three associates who remained were bound to him only by voluntary ties, they might quit him at any time. And soon a terrible war increased the loneliness and difficulty of his position.

It had often been asserted by the Legate, Pierre de Castelnau, that religion would never re-flourish in Languedoc until that country had been watered by a martyr's blood, and he earnestly besought God to allow him to be the victim. His petition was granted. He went to St. Gilles, at the pressing invitation of the Count of Toulouse, who expressed himself most anxious to make his peace with the Church. The Abbot de Cîteaux accompanied his colleague, both of them extremely desirous that the interview might result in peace. But the Count had acted hypocritically, intending really to compel them to free him from the ban of excommunication; for he threatened the Legates with death, if they dared quit St. Gilles without absolving him. The Legates despised his menaces, and withdrew, under protection of an escort given to them by the magistrates of the town. They spent the night on the banks of the Rhone, and on the following morning, having dismissed their escort, they prepared to cross the river; then two men approached, one of whom pierced Pierre de Castelnau with a lance. The Legate, mortally wounded, addressed his murderer in these words, "May God forgive you, even as I do."[1] This he repeated many times; exhorted his companions to serve the Church courageously and unweariedly, and then expired. His body was removed to the Abbey of St. Gilles: he was assassinated on the 17th January 1208.

This murder was the signal for the outbreak of a war in which Dominic took no part, and which was the source of great affliction to him in the exercise of his apostolate. As, however, the events of this war are interwoven with those of his life, it becomes necessary for me rapidly to trace its history.

---

[1] Pierre de Vaulx-Cernay, *Histoire des Albigeois*, ch. viii.

CHAPTER V.

The Albigensian War.[1]

W AR IS THE ACT by which a people resists injustice, at the price of its own blood. Wherever there is injustice, there also is a legitimate cause for war. Next to religion, war ranks as the first of earthly duties: one teaches us in what right consists, the other defends it; one is the word of God, the other is His arm. Holy, holy, holy, is the Lord God of hosts; that is, the God of justice; the God who sends forth the mighty to the succour of the poor oppressed; the God who hurls lofty powers in the dust; who raised up Cyrus for the overthrow of Babylon; who, for the people's sake, destroys the gates of brass, and brings destruction on the oppressor. But even as with the holiest things, so war itself may be perverted from its lawful end, and become the instrument of oppression; therefore, to judge of the character of any particular war, we must first know its object. Every war of deliverance is sacred, every war of oppression

---

[1] The chief contemporary historians of the Albigensian war are Pierre de Vaulx-Cernay, Cistercian monk, and Guillaume de Puys-Laurens, chaplain to Count Raymond VII. The *Recueil des Lettres d'Innocent III.* contains much valuable information on this head. See also *L'Histoire Générale du Languedoc*, by the Benedictines of Saint Maur, and *L'Histoire du Pape Innocent III., et de ses Contemporains*, by Hurter, President of the Consistory of Schaffhausen.

is cursed.

Until the era of the Crusades, almost the only cause that unsheathed and sanctified the sword, was the defence of the individual territory and government of each nation. The soldier died on the frontiers of his native land, and her name it was that inspired his heart in the moment of battle. But so soon as Gregory VII. had awakened in the mind of his contemporaries the idea of a Christian Republic, then the horizon of self-devotion widened with that of fraternity. Europe, one in faith, felt, no matter who the oppressor might be, that every oppressed Catholic nation had a right to her aid and her sword. Chivalry sprang into existence; war became not only a Christian, but also a monastic duty; and battalions of monks, clad in hair-cloth and shield, defended the outposts of the West. Every Christian clearly recognised himself as the instrument of right against might; and as the child of Him who heeds the faintest groan of His creatures, he too must be ever ready at the first cry of distress. Even as the hunter, ready for the chase, stands at the foot of a tree, intently listening to know from which point the wind blows, so Europe, then, lance in rest, and foot in stirrup, listened attentively to know from what quarter the cry of injury came. Whether it proceeded from a throne, or from a simpler dwelling; whether the sea must be traversed, or only a horse mounted in order to reach it; time, place, peril, rank, all were unheeded. They stayed not to count the gain or loss: blood gives itself gratuitously, or not at all. Conscience rewards it on earth, God repays it in heaven.

Among the causes which Christian chivalry had taken under her protection, was one most sacred of all; that of the Church. Having neither soldiers nor ramparts for her defence, she was always at the mercy of her persecutors, and of any hostile prince; but when chivalry arose, it took the City of God under its guard, because she needed protection, and because the cause of her liberty was the cause of mankind at large. As one oppressed, the Church had the same right as others to the aid of chivalry; as an institution founded by Jesus Christ, in order that she might carry on the work of enfranchising and saving mankind, the Church was Mother, Spouse, and Sister of all whose heart was noble, and whose sword was good. I like to believe that there is no one at the present day but can fully appreciate this sentiment; and that, amid all her misery, the glory of our age is, to know that there are wider and loftier claims than those of family and of nation. Sympathy makes nations go forth to aid each other, and the voice of the oppressed finds an echo in the world. What Frenchman is there who, if he could not in person, would not, at least, with his good wishes, accompany an army marching to the relief of Poland? What Frenchman, unbelieving though he may be, who does not rank among the greatest injustices done to that illustrious country, the violence shown to her religion, the exile of her priests and her bishops, the spoliation of her monasteries, the desecration of her churches, the torture of consciences? If the despotic arrest and imprisonment of the Archbishop of Cologne has caused so deep an emotion throughout modern Europe, what must not the Europe of the thirteenth century have experienced, in learning that an Apostolic Legate had just been treacherously assassinated?

Neither was this the first act of oppression for which Christendom had to demand satisfaction from the Count of Toulouse; for a long time there had been no safety for the Catholics in his dominions. The monasteries had been laid waste, the churches pillaged, and many of them turned into fortresses; he had expelled from their sees the Bishops of Carpentras and Vaison; a Catholic could obtain no redress; all the heretical undertakings were placed under his protection, and he manifested for religion that striking contempt which, in a prince, is synonymous with tyranny. One day when the Bishop of Orange came to entreat him to spare the consecrated edifices, and to abstain at least on Sundays and holy days from his hostile course, he seized the Bishop's hand and said: "I swear by this hand to take no note of Sundays or holy days, and to show no mercy either to persons or sacred things."[1]

France was at this time overrun by a number of unemployed soldiers, who, having formed themselves into several bands, filled the land with murder and rapine. Pursued by Philip Augustus, they could always take shelter with impunity in the territory of his vassal, the Count of Toulouse, and this on account of the service they rendered him by their depredations and sacrilegious acts of violence. They carried off the sacred vessels from the tabernacles;

---

[1] *Lettres d'Innocent III.*, book x. letter 69.

profaned the Body of our Lord; tore the ornaments from the images of the saints, to bestow them on abandoned women; laid the churches even with the ground; priests were beaten to death, many were skinned alive, and the execrable treachery of the prince left his subjects at the mercy of these persecuting assassins. When, then, after so many crimes of which he was either the author or accomplice, the Count of Toulouse had received the murderer of Pierre de Castelnau into the ranks of his friends, and loaded him with favours, the measure of his iniquity was full; the moment had come in which tyranny had become enfeebled by her own excesses.

It must not be imagined that it was an easy thing for Christendom to call the Count of Toulouse to account. His position was a strong one, as the sequel will prove. Raymond VI., after fourteen years of war, died victorious over his enemies; he transmitted his patrimony to his son, who enjoyed it during his life, and this important fief was only united to the French crown by the marriage between a brother of St. Louis and the only daughter of Count Raymond VII. The strength of this house resulted from many causes; it was of great antiquity, and a well-earned reputation had won for it the love of the people. Heresy, become almost universal, had formed between prince and people a new tie, which in separating them from the rest of Christendom gave their union the force of a religious league. Vassals of all grades shared the heresies of their suzerain, and the eager desire of obtaining the goods of the clergy added to community of sentiment community of interest also. The few

Catholics who remained were neither fervent enough nor numerous enough to weaken in any great measure this union, of which the Count was the head. Moreover, he had as faithful allies in his cause, the Counts of Foix and Comminges, Viscomte de Béarn, the King of Aragon, Pedro II., whose sister he had espoused, and he feared nothing from Guienne, which was then in the hands of the English. His suzerain, Philip-Augustus, at that time fully occupied by his quarrels with England and the empire, could not head the Crusade; and without such a leader, the only one then capable of inspiring fear, the army of Crusaders, composed of discordant elements, could only promise themselves transient victories, and a dissolution yet more speedy than their defeat. Master of the whole line of the Pyrenees, protected on the west by Aragon, on the right and left by the sea, and immediately surrounded by a number of fortified cities defended by faithful vassals, Count Raymond's chance of success was a thousandfold greater than that of his enemies. The Albigensian war was therefore a very serious one, and one in which the strategic difficulties were far outweighed by the moral ones; for what was to be done with the country even if it were conquered? We shall see the fine and noble soul of Innocent III. keenly alive to the danger of the position, and a mighty captain, victorious at the outset, succumbing to the weight of affliction, ere meeting with a soldier's death.

As soon as Innocent III. had been apprised of the assassination of Pierre de Castelnau, he wrote to the nobles, counts, barons, and chevaliers of Narbonne,

Arles, Embrun, Aix, and Vienne, and after eloquently describing his Legate's death, declared the Count of Toulouse excommunicated, his vassals and subjects absolved from their oath of allegiance, and his person and territories placed under the ban of Christendom, at the same time leaving open a door of reconciliation, in case the Count should repent and desire to make his peace with the Church. This letter is dated 10th March 1208. The Sovereign Pontiff also wrote in similar terms to the Archbishops and Bishops of the same provinces; to the Archbishop of Lyons, the Archbishop of Tours, and to the King of France.[1] To his only surviving Legate he associated Navarre, Bishop of Conserans, and Hugues, Bishop of Riez, specially charging the Abbot of Cîteaux to join with his monks in preaching the crusade. The rest of the year and the following spring were spent in making preparations.

Meanwhile, alarmed at what was going on, and knowing that the Bishops of the province of Narbonne had deputed their colleagues of Toulouse and Conserans to inform the Pope of the woes of their churches, Count Raymond sent the Archbishop of Auch, and the former Bishop of Toulouse, Rabenstens, on his own behalf to Rome. It was their duty to complain bitterly of the conduct of the Abbot of Cîteaux, and to assure the Sovereign Pontiff that their master was ready to make his submission and render full satisfaction to the Holy See, as soon as

---

[1] Book xi. letters 26, 27, and 28.

they would accord him more equitable Legates. Innocent III. consented to this, and despatched the apostolic notary, Milon (a man of consummate prudence), to France, in order that he might hear and judge the Count's cause. Milon convoked an assembly of bishops at Valence, where Raymond having presented himself, accepted the proposed conditions of peace, which were these: that he should expel the heretics from his territories; remove the Jews from all public offices; make compensation for the damage done to the monasteries and churches; re-establish in their sees the Bishops of Carpentras and Vaison; see to the security of the highways; exact no tax contrary to the ancient usage of the country; and purge his domains of the armed bands by which they were infested.

As a pledge of his good faith Raymond gave the Count of Melgueil as hostage to the Legate, together with the towns belonging to him in Provence, on condition of forfeiting them if he failed to keep his word. It was arranged that the reconciliation should take place at St. Gilles, with the accustomed forms. Had the Count of Toulouse been sincere, the open penitence to which he submitted, far from lowering him in the eyes of his contemporaries and of posterity, would have given him a right to the esteem of every Christian. The glory of Theodosius was not sullied by his permitting St. Ambrose to bar his entrance to the cathedral at Milan. It is only crime that dishonours; and voluntary expiation, especially in a sovereign, is a homage rendered to God and to man, exalting him who is capable of such expiation, and rendering him partaker of the invincible glory of the Crucified. Perchance my words are incomprehensible to pride, but what of that? The Cross has long reigned over the world, and pride has not yet divined the reason why. Let us leave this stone-blind one, and to those who will listen we will repeat the words of Him who, by voluntary submission to suffering, has conquered earth and heaven: *"Whosoever shall exalt himself shall be humbled: he that shall humble himself shall be exalted."* [1] So great is the power of misfortune, that had the Count of Toulouse been sincere, the penance to which he submitted would have won him universal sympathy. But the Count of Toulouse was not acting with sincerity; policy alone, extorted from him promises which he did not intend to fulfil, and when, having sworn by the relics of the saints, and by the Host itself, to observe all his promises, he presented himself at the gates of the Abbey of St. Gilles, offering his naked back to the scourges of the Legate, it was but a disgraceful scene of perjury and of ignominy. That which the most urgent necessity would have failed to justify, this man allowed with impunity. One memorable circumstance aggravated his punishment and rendered it the more striking. On attempting to quit the church, the crowd was so great that he could not advance a single step, therefore they let him through a secret door which gave access to the crypt, and he passed, naked and mangled, in front of the tomb of Pierre de Castelnau.

---

[1] St. Matthew xxiii. 12.

A few days after this event, which occurred on 18th June 1209, the Legate, Milon, rejoined the army of the Crusaders at Lyons. It was commanded by the Duke of Burgundy, the Counts of Nevers, and of St. Paul, Bar and Montfort, many other noblemen of distinction, and some few Prelates. In case of the absolution of the Count of Toulouse, Innocent III. had ordered that they should leave his domains unmolested; but that they should march against his vassals and allies, in order to compel their submission. The army therefore advanced in the direction of Languedoc, but had hardly reached Valence, when Count Raymond came forth to meet them, also wearing the Cross. They laid siege to Béziers, which having been unexpectedly taken by assault, fell a victim to the fury of the soldiery, without distinction of age, sex, or religion. The Legates, in their letters to the Sovereign Pontiff, computed the number of killed to be nearly twenty thousand, and this unforeseen and unwished-for carnage is one of those events which have invested the Albigensian war with a character that no historian can efface. The taking of Carcassonne almost immediately followed that of Béziers; the inhabitants surrendered and were spared, but the town was given up to premeditated pillage. It was hardly possible to commence more unfortunately a war so just in principle.

Up to this moment the Abbot of Cîteaux was the soul and the leader of the Crusade; after the successes at Béziers and Carcassonne, the Crusaders, of whom many meditated a retreat, resolved on electing a military chief. The choice being intrusted to the

decision of a council, composed of the Abbot of
Cîteaux, of two bishops and of four knights, they
deemed none worthier of the command than Count
Simon de Montfort. This warrior was descended
from the house of Hainault; he was the offspring of
the marriage of Simon III., Count of Montfort and
Evreux, with a daughter of Robert, Earl of Leicester,
and he had espoused Alice de Montmorency, a
woman as heroic as her name. No braver soldier or
more pious knight could be found than the Count of
Montfort, and had he but united to these eminent
personal qualities more disinterestedness and more
gentleness, none of the Eastern Crusaders would
have surpassed him in renown. Hardly was he appointed to the general command than he beheld
himself left almost alone. The Count of Nevers, the
Count of Toulouse, and the Duke of Burgundy withdrew, one after the other, leaving Montfort with
about thirty knights and a small number of soldiers.
This was a change of fortune incidental to such expe-
ditions, of which the members came and went
according to their own good pleasure.

I need scarcely remark that I intend but to trace
the general outline of the war and its attending negotiations; the clue is not easy to find, inasmuch as
two parties disputed the direction,—that of the Abbot of Cîteaux and that of the Pope.

The plan of the Abbot of Cîteaux, in conjunction
with the chief bishops of Languedoc and the neighbouring provinces, was totally to destroy the House
of Toulouse. This was both unjust and impolitic. It
was unjust; for if Raymond VI. merited destruction,

and the suspicion in which he was held, it was not so with his son, a child twelve years old, who was neither an accomplice in his father's crimes, nor incapable of Christian training under proper tutelage. It was impolitic, inasmuch as a religious question, regarding which there was unity of opinion throughout Christendom, was now involved with a party question tending to promote disunion. It also gave an ambitious hue to a war undertaken from the purest motives. It is true that in the Count de Montfort, the Abbot of Cîteaux had the rare good fortune to meet with a man exactly fitted for the work; and this may possibly have decided the Abbot to effect the annihilation of the House of Toulouse. The Count of Montfort's martial qualities could but prove adverse to the subjects and vassals of that house, and the Abbot, anxious to make prompt use of the forces of the crusade, overlooked the facts that time was required in order to substitute a new line for that of the old reigning one; also he should have feared transforming a war undertaken in the interests of Catholicism, into a mere party war between the House of Raymond and that of Montfort. To the abuse of his authority in furthering this unwise scheme, the errors and outrages are to be attributed, which robbed the crusade against the Albigenses of the sanctity of character otherwise attaching to it.

Innocent III. was a man totally different to the Abbot of Cîteaux; moreover, he was seated on that privileged throne which, besides the eternal aid of the Holy Spirit, has in virtue of its exaltation, the advantage of being superior to those passions which too

often mingle with the noblest cause. Whilst rash zeal
too often aims at destroying the individual with the
heresy, the Papacy always strives to save the individual by the destruction of the heresy. Innocent III.
had no wish to exterminate the House of Toulouse,
neither did he despair of awakening in Raymond
feelings more worthy of his ancestral line. In the letters of excommunication fulminated against the
Count, the possibility of his repentance had not been
overlooked, and the Pope had strictly enjoined that
the Count's territory should be unmolested. But
there were none in France ready to second the Holy
Father's generous intentions; he could not withstand
the force of events, and his efforts, though fruitless,
have shed additional lustre on his memory. Count
Raymond, by departing from the pacific course he
had at first adopted, also contributed to the success
of his foes, and it needed a mighty arm to change the
current of affairs.

Though left with but a handful of followers, Montfort continued to advance, storming, losing, and
retaking towns; whilst the Count of Toulouse, secure
in his reconciliation with the Church, appeared unmoved by the loss of his vassals and allies. A council
held at Avignon by the Metropolitans of Vienne, Aries, Embrun, and Aix, under the presidency of the
two Legates, Hugues and Milon, roused him from his
lethargy. The Council, opened on the 16th of September 1208, granted him a delay of six weeks, in which,
under pain of excommunication, he was to fulfil the
promises made by him at St. Gilles. On hearing this,
Raymond set out for Rome, and on being granted an

audience of the Holy Father, who received him with
many marks of affection, complained of the severity
with which he had been treated by the Legates; produced authentic testimony respecting several
churches that he had indemnified; and declared himself ready to observe the remainder of his oaths, at
the same time asking permission to be allowed to ex-
onerate himself from the murder of Pierre de
Castelnau, and from the charge of carrying on com-
munications with the heretics. The Pope encouraged
him in these sentiments; and commanded that a
fresh council of Bishops should assemble in France
in order to hear his justification, with the express
clause, that, if found guilty, his sentence should be
reserved for the Holy See. On leaving Rome, Raymond visited the Imperial Court, and that of France,
hoping to obtain assistance, but in vain; he was
therefore obliged to appear before the Council appointed to try his cause, and which was to be held at
St. Gilles about the middle of September in the year
1210. He wished to clear himself of the double charge
of holding communication with the heretics and of
being an accomplice in the assassination of Pierre de
Castelnau; but the Council refused him audience on
these two points, simply requesting that he would
keep his word and purge his domains of the heretics
and miscreants with which they abounded. Raymond could not, or would not, comply with this
demand, and returned to Toulouse fully convinced
that artifice was of no further avail, and that henceforth he could hope for nothing save from the chance

of war. The Council refrained from excommuni-
cating him, inasmuch as the Sovereign Pontiff had
reserved the right of pronouncing the final sentence,
and Innocent III. contented himself with writing an
urgent and affectionate letter, abstaining from all
menace and exhorting him to carry his promises into
effect.[1]

The King of Aragon also used his influence in order to prevent a final rupture, and two conferences
were held in the winter of the year 1211, one at Narbonne, and the other at Toulouse. In the first of these
the Count openly refused the conditions already proposed to him at St, Gilles, in the second, after
apparently giving his consent, he abruptly withdrew.
The King of Aragon, irritated at such behaviour, betrothed his son to a daughter of the Count de
Montfort, both children being at that time about
three years of age. The boy was intrusted to the care
of the Count in order that he might be trained under
his direction; but Pedro soon regretted this step, and
gave his sister in marriage to Count Raymond's only
son, thus strengthening the bond, already too firm,
which united him to the heretical party.

Finally, the Abbot of Cîteaux launches the excommunication and sends an envoy to the Pope in order
to obtain its confirmation; Innocent III. confirms it.
Raymond, first assuring himself of the fealty of his
subjects and the assistance of the Counts of Foix and
of Comminges, and of many other nobles, prepares

---

[1] Book xiii. letter 88.

for war. He repulses Montfort, who had appeared before the walls of Toulouse; the Albigensian army
encamps before Castelnandary; a sanguinary battle
ensues, and Raymond is forced to raise the siege.
The Crusaders win the day. Town after town falls
into their hands; the territories of Foix and Commin-
gles are invaded, and Raymond proceeds to Spain to
implore aid from the King of Aragon.

Subsequent events prove how perplexed and tried
the Pope then was. The King of Aragon, before arm-
ing in his brother-in-law's defence, thought it best to
try once more the result of negotiation, and sent an
embassy to the Sovereign Pontiff, complaining not
only of the Count of Montfort, who had seized some
of his fiefs, but also of the Apostolic Legates, who pos-
itively refused to admit the Count of Toulouse to
penance. On hearing this, Innocent III. wrote to his
Legates, reproaching them for their conduct, and
commanding them to summon a council of the bishops and nobles of the country, in order to decide on
the best measures for securing peace.[1] He ordered
Count Montfort to restore the fiefs belonging to the
King of Aragon and his vassals, "lest," said he, "it
should be thought that the Count had fought more
from motives of personal interest than in defence of
the faith."[2] He then resolved to suspend the Crusade, and wrote a private letter to this effect,
addressed to the Abbot of Cîteaux, then, and for some
time previously, Archbishop of Narbonne.[3] But

---

[1] Book xv. letter 211.
[2] Ibid. 215.
[3] Ibid. 215.

whilst these letters, dated early in the year 1213, were on their way, a council had assembled at Lavaur, at the request of the King of Aragon, who had sent written entreaties, begging the Legates and Bishops to restore the territories belonging to the Counts of Toulouse, Comminges, and Foix, also those of the Vicomte de Béarn, and to re-admit them into communion with the Church, on such terms as the Legates and Bishops might think fit. In case of refusal on the part of the Count of Toulouse, the King begged the council to do justice to the son. The decision of the council was, that the Count of Toulouse having so often violated his word, could be allowed no further hearing, but that the Counts of Foix and Comminges, and the Vicomte de Béarn, would be admitted to penance as soon as they should desire it. Concluding from this reply that there was a fixed determination to overthrow the House of Toulouse, the King of Aragon loudly declared, that from the inexorable severity of the Legates and Bishops he would appeal to the clemency of the Holy See, and take Raymond and his son beneath his own royal protection. No suspicion of heresy can attach itself to this prince; he had surrendered his kingdom as apostolic fief of the Holy See, and had valiantly defended Christendom in her struggle with the Moors of Spain. All was imperilled by the weight of his name and sword; therefore the Council of Lavaur hastened to despatch four envoys to the Sovereign Pontiff, with a letter, the aim of which was to persuade him that unless the Count of Toulouse and his heirs were deprived of their territories, the Catholic cause would be lost.

The Archbishops of Aries, Aix, and Bordeaux, the Bishops of Maguelonne, Carpentras, Orange, St. Paul-Trois-Châteaux, Cavaillon, Vaison, Bazas, Béziers, and Perigueux, wrote in the same strain to the Holy Father. Innocent III. complained of having been deceived by the King of Aragon; commanded him to desist from his undertaking, conclude a truce with the Count de Montfort, and await the arrival of the Cardinal, whom he was about to despatch to those parts.[1] But the die was cast. The King assembled an army in Catalonia and Aragon, and crossing the Pyrenees, united his troops to those of the Counts of Toulouse, Foix, and Comminges.

Montfort was at Fanjeaux, when he learnt that the allied army, consisting of 40,000 infantry and 2000 horse, was advancing in the direction of Muret, an important place, situated on the Garonne, three leagues from Toulouse. This was the sublime moment in his life. He had at his disposal only about 800 horse and a small number of foot soldiers; he set out at once for Muret, early in the day, accompanied by his men-at-arms, and by the Bishops of Toulouse, Nîmes, Uzès, Lodève, Béziers, Agde, Comminges, and by three Cistercian Abbots. Arriving the same day at the Cistercian monastery of Bolbonne, he entered the church, passed some time in prayer, and having deposited his sword on the altar, took it again into his hands, saying: "O Lord, who, unworthy as I am, hast chosen me to make war in Thy name, I take my sword back to-day from this altar, that in so doing

---

[1] Book xvi. letter 48.

I may receive my arms from Thee, in whose cause I
go forth to fight!"[1] He then marched to Saverdun,
where he passed the night. Next day he made his
confession, wrote his will, which he sent to the Abbot
of Bolbonne, praying him, in case of death, to transmit it to the Sovereign Pontiff. In the evening of the
same day, he crossed the Garonne without receiving
any interruption, and found himself close to the walls
of Muret, guarded only by thirty of his knights. This
was Wednesday, 12th September 1213. Before setting foot within the town, he had been rejoined by the
Bishops, who had quitted him for a moment in order
to sue for peace; but the King of Aragon had replied
that it was needless that a King and Bishops should
confer regarding a mere handful of soldiers. In spite
of the non-success of this attempt, when morning
arose the Bishops commissioned one of the monks to
notify to the King that they and all the Religious Orders would proceed barefooted, to implore him to
come to a more merciful decision. How bitterly the
Count of Toulouse must then have regretted his per-
juries and humiliations, all of which were fruitless!
How must he have blamed himself for not having had
recourse to a loyal and courageous war, instead of al-
lowing his friends to be crushed and his own cause
overwhelmed with dishonour! He had indeed deceived himself; as artifice, so was war destined to
prove destructive to him. God saw this prince's
heart, and felt no pity for his fate.

The Bishops were preparing to leave Muret in

---

[1] Pierre de Vaulx-Cernay, *Histoire des Albigeois*, ch. lxxi.

guise of suppliants, when a body of hostile knights hastened towards the gates. Montfort ordered his men to place themselves in battle array in the lower part of the town; and after praying in a church where the Bishop of Uzès was offering the Holy Sacrifice, donned his own armour; then, when equipped, he re-entered the church. As he knelt, the bands which fastened the lower parts of his armour broke in twain, and it was observed that as he set his foot in the stirrup, the charger tossed back his head and wounded him; but though men of his temperament are usually susceptible to such omens, the knight heeded them not. He rejoined his troops, followed by Foulques, Bishop of Toulouse, bearing the Crucifix in his hands. The knights dismounted in order to adore their Lord and kiss His sacred image; but the Bishop of Comminges, seeing that time pressed, took the Crucifix from Foulques, and standing on an elevated spot, made a brief harangue to the army, and blessed it. After this, all the ecclesiastics then present withdrew to the church to pray, and Montfort, at the head of 800 horse, quitted the town.

The ranks of the allies were drawn up in line, on a plain west of the town; Montfort, having issued by an opposite gate, as if he wished to flee, divided his forces into three squadrons, and made straight for the enemy's centre. After God, he placed his hopes on being able to break the lines of the confederates, and by the boldness of the attack, throw them into a state of terror and confusion, and profit by all those chances which, at such a moment, the eye of a great

captain knows how to discern. His hopes were realised. The first squadron broke through the enemy's
vanguard; the second penetrated to the hindmost
ranks, where the King of Aragon and the élite of his
army were stationed; Montfort, following closely
with the third squadron, attacked the bewildered Ar-
agonese in the flank. Fortune wavered a while, and
time was precious, for the battalions through whose
ranks a passage had been so happily made, were rather dazed than defeated, and might overwhelm
Montfort in the rear. A blow that unhorsed and
killed the King of Aragon, decided the day. The Ara-
gonese shout and flee, and the rest follow their
example. The Bishops, anxiously praying in the
church of Muret, some of them prostrated on the
pavement, others raising their hands to heaven, are
soon drawn to the walls by the sound of victory, and
behold the plain covered with fugitives fleeing before
the terrible arm of the Crusaders. A body of troops,
endeavouring to take the town by assault, throw
down their arms and are cut to pieces in their flight.
Montfort, returning from the pursuit of the vanquished, in traversing the field of battle beholds the
corpse of the King of Aragon extended on the ground,
already stripped and bare. He dismounts, and weeping, kisses the mangled remains of this unhappy
prince. Pedro II., king of Aragon, was a brave knight,
beloved by his subjects, a sincere Catholic, and worthy of a better death. The ties which united his two
sisters to the two Raymonds, had induced him to defend a cause, regarded by him as no longer one of
heresy, but one of justice and relationship. He fell by

a secret judgment of God, perhaps for having despised the supplications of the Bishops, and for
having, in heart, already made ill use of a victory regarded by him as certain. After providing for his
burial, Montfort entered Muret, barefooted, went to
the church to render God thanks for His protection,
and bestowed his horse and armour on the poor. This
memorable battle, fruit of a conscience that believed
firmly it was fighting in the cause of God, will ever
rank among the noblest acts of faith.

Dominic was at Muret with the seven Bishops and
the three Cistercian monks already named. Some
modern historians assert that he headed the combatants, Cross in hand, and they even showed in the
Inquisition at Toulouse, a Cross, pierced with ar-
rows, and said to be the one borne by him at the
battle of Muret. Contemporary historians relate
nothing of the sort; on the contrary, they affirm that
Dominic, with the Bishops and monks, remained in
the town engaged in prayer; and one of his biographers, Bernard Guidomo, who lived in the
Inquisition at Toulouse from 1308 to 1322, makes no
mention of the Crucifix, shown later on.

The battle of Muret gave a death-blow to the cause
of the Count of Toulouse, His allies, and the people of
his capital, tendered their submission to the Sovereign Pontiff, who commissioned Cardinal Pierre de
Bénévent to reconcile them to the Church, and compel Count de Montfort to send back to Spain the new
King of Aragon, the young child retained as hostage
since his betrothal to the Count's daughter. This
double mission was fulfilled by the Cardinal during

the winter of 1214, and, strange to relate, he even
gave absolution to the Count of Toulouse, but this act
of mercy availed not as regarded the temporal interests of the latter. In December following a council
assembled at Montpellier to decide to whom the sovereignty of the conquered territories should pertain.
The council decided unanimously in favour of the
Count de Montfort, whose strong and glittering
sword had turned the tide of war. Nevertheless, the
Sovereign Pontiff, in a letter of the 17th of April
1215,[1] declared that Montfort should only retain his
conquests until the Lateran Œcumenic Council—to
which the Pope referred the decision—should have
pronounced its final sentence. This was a last effort
made by Innocent III. to save the unhappy House of
Toulouse. Count Raymond, deserted by all, had
withdrawn with his son to the English court.

The sun, as it rose above the crest of the Apennines on the 11th November 1215, shone on the most
august assembly in the whole world, then reunited
within the church of St. John Lateran. Seated there
were 71 Primates and Metropolitans, 412 Bishops,
more than 800 Abbots and Priors, numerous representatives of absent Bishops and Abbots. The
ambassadors of the King of the Romans; of the Emperor of Constantinople; of the kings of France,
Hungary, Aragon, Jerusalem, and Cyprus; the envoys of a countless number of princes, nobles, and
municipalities, and above them all was seen the venerable form of Pope Innocent III. The Abbot of

---

[1] Vide *Conciles de Labbe*, t. xiii. p. 888.

Cîteaux, Archbishop of Narbonne, was there, and
Count Simon de Montfort was represented by his
brother, Guy de Montfort. The two Raymonds were
also there in person, likewise the Counts of Foix and
Comminges. On the day appointed to hear the grand
cause of the Albigensian crusade, the two Raymonds
entered the assembly, accompanied by the Counts of
Foix and Comminges, and prostrated themselves at
the foot of the Apostolic throne. Having risen, they
stated that they had been deprived of their fiefs, notwithstanding their entire submission to the Holy
See, and the absolution bestowed on them by the
Legate, Pierre de Bénévent. A cardinal then rose,
and spoke with much force and eloquence on their
behalf, as also the Abbot of St. Tiberius, and the
Chanter of the church at Lyons, of whom the latter
appeared to make great impression on the Holy Father. But the majority of the Bishops, especially the
French ones, pronounced against the suppliants, pro-
testing that should their estates be restored to them,
the Catholic cause in Languedoc would be doomed,
and the blood and zeal expended on its behalf would
all have been given in vain. The council declared
Count Raymond VI. to have forfeited his fiefs, which
were then finally transferred to the Count de Montfort, and a pension of four hundred marks was
assigned him on condition that he would live out of
his former territories; his wife Eléonore was to retain
her dowry; the Marquisate of Provence was reserved
for their son Raymond, to be handed over to him on
attaining his majority, if he remained faithful to the
Church. As for the Counts of Foix and Comminges,

their cause was deferred for further examination. It is worthy of remark, that the Marquisate of Provence, destined for young Raymond, consisted of the towns forfeited to the Holy See by the non-observance, on his father's part, of the treaty of St. Gilles. It had often been proposed that the Sovereign Pontiff should unite them to the territory of the Holy See, but the Pope never would consent to this, and the only use he made of the rights he had acquired was to retain these towns for the House of Toulouse. At the close of the council young Raymond, whose noble behaviour had won universal esteem, went to take leave of the Holy Father. He did not dissimulate his conviction that he was unjustly deprived of his ancestral patrimony, and naively and respectfully asserted that he should seize every opportunity of gloriously recovering that, which had been lost by no fault of his. Innocent III., touched by the innocence and courage of this youth of eighteen, gave him this prophetic benediction: "My son, in all your actions may you begin well, and end still better!" [1]

Montfort, invested by Philip Augustus with the titles of Duke of Narbonne and Count of Toulouse, did not long enjoy the power he had so laboriously acquired. Before the close of 1216, young Raymond had made himself master of a part of Provence; and Toulouse, wearied of the yoke of its new master, recalled old Raymond from the English court where he had fled for refuge, and opened its gates to him. At the first intimation of a change of fortune a number of

[1] *Histoire Générale du Languedoc*, t. iii.

nobles hastened to swear fealty to their former suzerain. Then the conqueror of Muret knew that martial renown alone will not ensure a people's allegiance; and, by his misfortune, learnt the lesson that he who would rule effectually, must reign in his subjects' hearts. Chased from Toulouse, after having disarmed and chastised it in vain, he sorrowfully laid siege to those walls within which he would never more re-enter. The length of the siege, the uncertainty of the future, the reproaches of inaction addressed to him by Cardinal Bertrand, the Apostolic Legate, joined to the depression reverses cause when they come late in life, threw the brave knight into such a state of melancholy, that he prayed God for death. Very early in the morning of the 25th June 1218, he was told that the foe was in ambush in the castle moat He called for his arms, and having equipped himself, went to hear Mass. When it was already commenced, they came to tell him that the engines of war were assailed and in danger of destruction. "Leave me," he rejoined, "that I may behold the Sacrament of our Redemption." Then another messenger arrived with the tidings that the troops could resist no longer. "I will not depart," he replied, "until I have seen my Saviour." Then when the priest had elevated the Sacred Host, Montfort, kneeling on the ground, with hands upraised to heaven, uttered these words, *Nunc Dimittis*, and set out. His presence on the field made the enemy retreat to the fosses surrounding the town; but this victory was his last. He was hit on the head by a stone, and striking his breast and recommending

himself to God and the Blessed Virgin, he fell down
dead.

Fortune continued to favour the Raymonds. Of
the two sons left by the Count de Montfort, the
younger was killed before the walls of Castelnandary. Four years of non-success convincing the elder
that he could not retain his father's heritage, he
ceded his rights to the King of France. Old Raymond
reposing at Toulouse, secure in his son's success, had
time to turn his thoughts to Him who had abased and
reexalted him. On the 12th July 1222, on returning
from the door of a church, for he was still excommunicated, he felt himself indisposed, and sent in haste
for the Abbot of Saint-Sernin that he might reconcile
him to the Church, The Abbot found him already
speechless. On beholding him, the old Count raised
his eyes to heaven, and taking the Abbot's hands in
his, grasped them till his last breath. His body was
removed to the church of the Knights of St. John of
Jerusalem, which he had chosen for his place of sepulture, but being excommunicated they dared not
inter him. He was therefore left in an open coffin,
and three hundred years after was still to be seen
there, no hand having been so daring as to nail a
plank on that bier hallowed by death and time. At
his son's request, the question of sepulture was discussed during the pontificates of Gregory IX. and
Innocent IV. Numerous witnesses asserted that before death he had given real signs of repentance; yet
men feared to disturb those ashes, by rendering them
a tardy homage.

Raymond VII. survived his father twenty-six

years. He withstood even the arms of France, but too feeble for the continued struggle, he concluded with St. Louis, in 1228, the treaty ending this long war. The chief conditions of peace were these: His only daughter was to be given in marriage to one of the King's brothers, the Count of Poitiers, with the reversion of the county of Toulouse, as her dowry; certain territories were to be ceded; he was to promise fidelity to the Church, and use his authority to suppress heresy. The Church confirmed this peace by restoring the young Count to her communion; and by way of penance, he promised to serve in Palestine for the space of five years. Twenty years later on, he seriously thought of fulfilling this duty, and set out for the Holy Land. But God arrested him on his way; he fell ill at Pris, near Rhodes, whence he was removed to Milhaud, and died there on the 26th September 1248, surrounded by the Bishops of Toulouse, Agen, Cahors, and Rhodes, the Consuls of Toulouse, and a number of nobles, all of whom had arrived to take a last leave of a prince whom they loved, and who was the last male representative of the elder branch of an illustrious race. On the Holy Viaticum being brought, the Count rose from his bed, and knelt in presence of his Lord, in death as in life, realising the wish expressed by Pope Innocent III., when he blessed him as a youth, in these words: "My son, in all your actions may you begin well, and end still better."

CHAPTER VI.

St. Dominic's Apostolate from the commencement of the Albigensian War until the close of the Fourth Lateran Council.—Institution of the Rosary.—St. Dominic and his first disciples.

T HE MOMENT of the outbreak of the Albigensian war, was the moment in which the whole force and genius of St. Dominic were brought to light. Two courses were before him, either to abandon his mission in a land then the scene of sanguinary conflict and alarm, or take part in the war as the Cistercian monks had done. In following either course, his destiny would have been unaccomplished; by fleeing, he would have been faithless to his apostolate; by taking part in the crusade, his labours and his life would have been shorn of their apostolic character; he therefore did neither the one nor the other. Toulouse being the headquarters of heresy in Europe, it behoved St. Dominic to fix his abode there, after the example of the Apostles, who, far from shunning the evil, invariably sought out its stronghold. St. Peter settled first at Antioch, queen of the Orient, and sent his disciple St. Mark to Alexandria, one of the first commercial cities in the world. St. Paul dwelt for some time at Corinth, renowned among the other cities of Greece both for its magnificence and for the depravity of its morals. And because Jesus Christ has said, "*It cannot be that a prophet perish out of Jerusalem*,"[1] St. Peter and St. Paul undesignedly met at Rome, *whither they had gone to die.* Therefore at Toulouse, the centre and focus of heresy, it behoved St. Dominic to pitch his tent. In the hour of alarm, men of weak faith shrink from action; but the apostle sows in the storm that he may reap in the calm. He remembers the words of his Master: "*You shall hear of wars and rumours of wars. See that ye be not troubled.*"[2] Still, while persevering in his mission despite the terrors of war, Dominic felt it more than ever incumbent on him not to deviate from the pacific and zealous course he had hitherto adopted. However justifiable it may be to draw the sword in the defence of truth when oppressed by violence, it is not easy to prevent truth suffering even by this very protection, nor is it easy to avoid making her an accomplice in the excesses inseparable from all sanguinary conflicts. The sword does not stay its course precisely at the line where justice ends, nor will it easily re-enter its sheath when once it has been heated in mortal strife. To fight on behalf of right, angelic combatants are needed, for, so fickle is the human heart, that even the oppressor, once vanquished, may hope for a share in its sympathy. Therefore was it of sovereign import that St. Dominic should faithfully carry out Azévédo's grand design, and that, side by side with chivalry armed in defence

---

[1] St. Luke xiii. 33.
[2] St. Matthew xxiv. 6.

of the Church's liberty, should be seen the Christian man trusting to the sole might of grace and of persuasion. In Poland, whilst the Priest at the Altar recited the Gospel, the Knight half unsheathed his sword, and in this warlike attitude listened to the gentle words of Christ,—type this, of the true mutual relations existing between the Church and the world. In her representative the Priest, the Church speaks, prays, consecrates and offers the Holy Sacrifice; the world, in its representative the Knight, listens in silence, sharing in all the acts of the Priest, holding its sword drawn, not to enforce the faith, but only to ensure its liberty.

In the mystery of Christianity, Priest and Knight have each their allotted sphere. Whilst the Priest sings the Gospel aloud, in presence of the people, and by the light of tapers, the Knight holds his sword half sheathed, because mercy speaks as well as justice; and the Gospel, in whose defence he holds himself in readiness, whispers to him these words: *"Blessed are the meek: for they shall possess the earth."* [1]

Dominic and Montfort were the two heroes of the Albigensian war, the one as Knight, the other as Priest. We have seen how Montfort fulfilled his task, we will now see how Dominic accomplished his. It will doubtless have been remarked that no mention is made of his taking part in the war. He is absent from councils, conferences, reconciliations, sieges and triumphs; and the letters from Rome make no allusion to him. We have only met him once, and

---

[1] St. Matthew v. 4.

that at Muret, praying in a church during the moment of battle. This general silence on the part of historians is so much the more significant, inasmuch as they belong to different schools, secular and religious; the latter, favourable to the Crusaders, and the former, partisans of Raymond. It is therefore highly improbable that historians would have vied in silence with each other, had Dominic taken any part either in the negotiations, or military deeds of the Crusade. They have chronicled his other actions, why then should these have been concealed? Here are the fragments they have preserved of his life at that time:—

"After Bishop Dingo's return to his diocese," says the Blessed Humbert, "St. Dominic, who had remained alone (save for a few companions, bound to him by no vow), for the space of ten years defended the Catholic faith in several parts of Narbonne, especially in Carcassonne and Fanjeaux. He wholly devoted himself to the salvation of souls, by the office of preaching; and willingly endured many affronts, and much ignominy and suffering, for the name of our Lord Jesus Christ."[1]

Dominic had selected Fanjeaux as his residence, because, from the eminence on which it was situated he could discern the convent of Notre-Dame-de-Prouille, in the plain below. As regards Carcassonne, also not far removed from that dear retreat, he has himself given another reason for his preference for it.

---

[1] *Chronique*, n. 2.

Questioned one day why he would not remain in Toulouse and its diocese, he replied, "Because much
honour is shown me in the diocese of Toulouse, whilst
at Carcassonne every one is adverse to me."[1] And the
enemies of the faith did indeed insult this servant of
God in every possible manner, spitting in his face,
pelting him with mud, and fastening straws to his
cloak. But, indifferent to all such treatment, he, like
the Apostle, esteemed himself happy in that he was
deemed worthy to suffer shame for the name of Jesus. The heretics even meditated taking his life, and
when once they threatened so to do, he replied, "I am
unworthy of martyrdom; I have not yet merited such
a death."[2] This is why, having to traverse a spot
where he knew they were lying in wait for him, he
went on his way fearlessly, singing gaily. Surprised
at his firmness, the heretics, in order to prove him,
asked him on another occasion what he would have
done had he fallen into their hands. "I should have
besought you," he replied, "not to kill me at a single
stroke, but to sever my members one by one, and after showing them to me, then to end by putting out
my eyes, leaving me half-dead, or killing me at your
pleasure."[3]

Thierry d'Apolda relates the following: An important conference being about to take place with the
heretics, a certain bishop prepared to attend in great
pomp; then the humble messenger of Christ said to
him, "Not so, my lord and father, must we act with

---

[1] Constantin d'Orviéto, *Vie de St. Dominique*, n. 44.

[2] Ibid. n. 44.

[3] Ibid. n. 12.

the children of pride. The foes of truth must be convinced by examples of humility, patience, religion, and every virtue, and not by the pomp of grandeur and outward, worldly show. Let us arm ourselves with prayer, and with external marks of humility advance barefooted to meet these Goliaths." The Bishop followed this pious counsel, and all bared their feet But not being quite sure which road they ought to take, they intrusted themselves to the guidance of a heretic whom they thought orthodox, and who promised to conduct them on their way; but he, actuated by malice, led them into a wood full of thorns and briars, which wounded their feet and covered them with blood. Then the strong man of God patiently and joyfully exhorted his companions to give thanks for these sufferings, saying to them, "Trust in the Lord, my well beloved; victory will be yours, for see, our sins are expiated by blood." The heretic, touched by the Saint's wondrous patience and words, confessed his wickedness and abjured heresy.[1]

In the vicinity of Toulouse were some women of noble birth who had been seduced from the faith by the outward show of austerity assumed by the heretics. In the intention of bringing them back to the Church, Dominic asked hospitality of them at the beginning of Lent. He entered on no controversy, but during the whole of Lent he and his companions took nothing but bread and water. When on the first

---

[1] *Vie de St. Dominique*, chap. ii. n. 35.

evening of their sojourn beds were about to be prepared for them, they asked for two planks instead,
and, until Easter, used no other bed, contenting
themselves nightly with only a short sleep, interrupted by prayer. This silent eloquence proved
irresistible; and their hostess acknowledged such abnegation to be the effect of love, and that where such
love existed, there was the true faith.

We recollect that at Palencia Dominic wished to
sell himself into captivity in order to ransom the
brother of a poor woman: in Languedoc he experienced a similar desire with regard to a heretic who
avowed that poverty was the sole cause of his remaining outside the Church. Dominic resolved on
selling himself in order to provide means of subsist-
ence for the poor man, and would have carried his
design into execution, had not Divine Providence
found other ways of accomplishing the same end.

Another fact, yet more singular, exhibits the inge-
nuity of Dominic's benevolence. "Some heretics,"
says Thierry d'Apolda, "having been taken and convicted in the province of Toulouse, were banded over
to the secular arm, and condemned to be burnt because they refused to return to the faith." Dominic,
gazing at one of them, his heart full of the secrets of
God, said to an officer of the court, "Set this man
aside, and beware of putting him to death." Then
turning to the heretic, addressed him with great gentleness, saying, "My son, I know that time is needed,
but one day you will be a saint." Marvellous and con-
soling prediction this! Twenty years this man
remained in heresy; but then, touched by divine

grace, begged admittance to the Order of Friar Preachers, in which order he led a, holy life, persevering even to the end."[1]

Constantin d'Orviéto and the Blessed Humbert, in relating the same occurrence, add one fact requiring some explanation. They say that the heretics in question had been *convicted* by Dominic before they were handed down to the secular arm. This is the sole word in the whole nineteenth century that can lead one to suppose that the Saint took any part in these proceedings at law. But the historians of the Albigensian war explain clearly what was meant by this *conviction* of heresy. In Languedoc the heretics did not form a secret society; they were armed, and fought openly in behalf of their tenets. When the fate of war had placed any of them in the power of the Crusaders, priests were sent to explain to them Catholic dogmas, and make them realise the unsoundness of their own. This was termed CONVINCING them, not of being heretics, for this they proclaimed themselves to be, but of being in a false road, one contrary to Scripture, tradition, and reason. They entreated them fervently to abandon their errors, promising them pardon in return. Such who did yield, were spared; those who finally resisted, were given over to the secular arm.

Convicting (or *convincing*) heretics was therefore a work demanding much devotedness, one in which the power of intellect and eloquence of love were kindled by the hope of saving the unhappy ones from

---

[1] *Vie de St. Dominique*, chap. iv. n. 34.

death. That such an office was filled, at least once, by St. Dominic, is beyond all doubt, since such is asserted by two contemporary historians; but to make that a ground for accusing him of dealing harshly with the heretics, would be to confuse the priest who assists a criminal, with the judge who condemns, or the executioner who puts him to death.

Astonishment may possibly be felt that Dominic should be able to spare a heretic's life, by means of a simple prediction; but not only did his renown for sanctity inspire confidence in his words, he had also been invested by the Apostolic Legates with power to reconcile heretics. The proof of this is to be found in two documents, which, though undated, refer to this epoch of his life. The one runs thus: "To all the faithful in Christ whom these letters shall reach, Brother Dominic, Canon of Osma, and humble preacher, sends greeting in the Lord. Be it known to you that we have permitted Raymond Guillaume d'Hauterive Pélagionire to receive Guillaume Huguecion into his house at Toulouse, without any danger or dishonour to himself; and we grant him this permission until the Lord Cardinal shall notify otherwise."[1] The other document is couched in these words: "To all the faithful in Christ whom these letters shall reach, Brother Dominic, Canon of Osma, sends greeting in the Lord. *In virtue of the authority given to us* by the Abbot of Cîteaux, we have reconciled to the Church, the bearer of the present letter, Ponce Roger, by God's

---

[1]   See Echard's *Ecrivains de l'Ordre des Prêcheurs*, vol. i. p. 9, note.

grace converted from heresy; and we enjoin, in virtue of the oath made to us by him, that he shall on three Sundays, or holy days, proceed from the outskirts of the village, to the church, bared to the waist and scourged by the priest. We also command him to abstain always from the use of flesh meat, eggs, and cheese, save at Easter, Pentecost, and Christmas, at which times he shall eat thereof by way of protest against his former errors. He shall observe three Lents yearly, fasting and abstaining from fish, unless bodily infirmity or the heats of summer render a dispensation necessary. He shall wear a monastic habit, to the outer edge of which two small crosses are to be attached. If possible, he must hear Mass daily, and on holy days attend Vespers. He is to recite seven Pater Nosters during the day, and twenty at midnight. He is to observe chastity, and once a month is to present this letter, in the morning, to the chaplain of the village of Céré, whom we enjoin to be careful that his penitent lead a good life, observing all our injunctions, until the Legate shall order otherwise. If he neglect the observance of these commands, he shall, as a perjurer and heretic, be excommunicated and cut off from the assembly of the faithful." [1]

If any one deem these injunctions either strange or severe, I refer him to the Canonical Penances enjoined by the Early Church; also to the penitential

---

[1]   See Echard's *Ecrivains de l'Ordre des Prêcheurs*, vol. i. p. 8, note.

discipline observed in the cloister, and to the voluntary and public penances submitted to in mediaeval
times by many Christians, in expiation of their sins.
One example will suffice. We all know how Henry
II., king of England, allowed himself to be scourged
by the monks at the tomb of Thomas à Becket, Archbishop of Canterbury, whose murder he had
instigated. In Rome, at the present day, the priests
in certain Basilicas, after absolving the penitent,
give him a stroke on the shoulder with the end of a
long rod. It was natural that St. Dominic should con-
form to the custom of the times; and, to any careful
reader, the above injunctions are replete with a spirit
of kindness.

His charity and gentleness were equalled only by
his disinterestedness; he refused the Sees of Béziers.
Conserans, and Comminges; and once declared that
rather than accept the episcopacy, or any other dignity, he would take his staff, and flee away during
the night.

Here is his portrait, sketched by the Abbot of a
monastery of Saint-Paul in France, Guillaume de
Pierre, who knew him intimately during his twelve
years' apostolate in Languedoc, and who was one of
the witnesses heard at Toulouse during the process
of canonisation: "The blessed Dominic had an ardent
thirst for souls, and his zeal on their behalf was un-
bounded. So fervent a prelate was he, that day and
night, at home and abroad, he ceased not to preach
the Word of God, counselling his brethren to do the
same, and to converse of nought save God. He was a
foe to heresy; opposing it in sermons, controversies,

and in every possible way. From love of poverty, he renounced all possessions, farms, chateaux and revenues, with which, in many localities, his Order had been endowed. So frugal was he, that his ordinary diet consisted of a piece of bread and some soup, save on rare occasions and out of respect for the brothers and guests, whose fare he desired should be as generous as circumstances would allow. I have heard it said by many that he was a virgin. He refused the See of Conserans, although duly elected. Never have I seen his equal in humility; nor any who so despised worldly glory and all pertaining thereto. Injuries, curses, and opprobrium, were welcomed by him as priceless gifts; he heeded not persecution, was unmoved in danger, and nothing could make him swerve from his course. When wearied with his journeys, he would take his rest on the ground, fearless of all danger. In piety, he surpassed all whom I have ever known; despised and counted himself as worthless; tenderly consoled his sick brethren, patiently bearing with their weakness. Those oppressed by anxiety, he exhorted to resignation, and did his best to comfort them. He loved the Rule, and paternally reproved those who were in fault; in all things he was an example to the brethren, both in word and deed. Never have I seen any one so continually given to prayer, or who had the gift of tears in such abundance. When praying, his cries could be heard afar, and he would exclaim, 'Lord, have mercy on the people, have mercy on those who sin.' He passed his nights without sleep, weeping and groaning for the transgressions of others; was generous and hospitable, willingly giving all he had unto the poor; he loved and honoured all who belonged to Christ, and those who were friends to religion. I have never heard of his having any other place of repose than the church, when he could find a church open; and if that failed him, then he lay on a bench or on the ground, or stripped the bed prepared for him, taking his rest on the sacking only. I have always seen him wear the same garment, full of patches; and his clothing was worse than that of any of his brethren. He loved peace and sincerity, and was a zealous promoter of both." [1]

The gift of miracles was also bestowed on Dominic together with these exalted virtues. One day, having crossed a river, the boatman demanded his fare, upon which Dominic replied, "I am a servant and disciple of Christ, and possess neither silver nor gold: God will compensate you for my debt." The boatman on hearing this, evinced extreme displeasure, and, seizing Dominic's garment, exclaimed, "Pay me my money, or give me this." Dominic raised his eyes to heaven, and after a moment's silence pointed to the ground, where lay a piece of money that Providence had just furnished, saying, "My brother, behold what you desire; take it, and let me go in peace."

Whilst the Crusaders were before Toulouse in the year 1211, some English pilgrims on their way to St. Iago de Compostello, wishing to avoid entering Toulouse, on account of the interdict under which it lay,

---

[1] *Actes de Toulouse*, n. 15.

took a boat, in order to cross the Garonne. There were more than forty of them, and the boat, being too full, sank. The shrieks of the pilgrims and soldiers brought Dominic out of a neighbouring church. He threw himself on the ground, extending his arms crosswise, imploring God on behalf of the drowning pilgrims. His prayer ended, he arose, and turning towards the bank of the river, said in a loud voice, "In the name of Christ I command you to come ashore."[1] Immediately they all appeared above the surface, and seizing the long pikes extended to them by the soldiers, came safe to land.

The first Prior of the monastery of Saint-Jacques de Paris, called by historians, Matthew of France, became a fellow-labourer with Dominic, so impressed was he by a miracle of which he was spectator. He was Prior at Castres, the church of which contained the relics of St. Vincent the Martyr, and was frequently visited by St. Dominic, who generally remained there until noon. Staying one day beyond his wonted time, the hour of the midday repast, the Prior sent one of the clerics in search of him. This one beheld Dominic before the altar, raised from the earth by the distance of half a cubit; he ran to tell the Prior, who finding Dominic in this ecstatic condition, was so deeply impressed, that he soon after associated himself to this servant of God, who, in conformity with his usual custom regarding all whom he admitted to a share in his labours, promised him *the Bread of Life, and the Dew of Heaven.*

---

[1] Thierry d'Apolda, *Vie de St. Dominique*, ch. iii. n. 48.

Historians briefly narrate the following:—His cur-
ing a man possessed by the devil; his desire to pray
in a certain church, the doors of which being closed,
he suddenly found himself transported within the edifice; his travelling with a monk, and though neither
understood the other's native tongue, they nevertheless conversed intelligibly for three days; his letting
his books fall into the river Ariégo, when a fisherman
drawing them out some time after, found them unin-
jured by the water. All these facts, floating isolated
and unconnected on the stream of history, are gathered together by us as sacred relics.

God also endowed His servant with the spirit of
prophecy, during the Lent of 1213, which he spent at
Carcassonne, preaching and fulfilling the duties of
Vicar-General, intrusted to him by the Bishop, during his absence. A Cistercian monk questioned him
as to the issue of the war. "Master Dominic," said he,
"will these woes never end?" And as Dominic remained silent, the monk repeated his question,
knowing that God revealed many things to His servant. At last Dominic replied, "Yes, these woes will
end, but not speedily; much blood will be shed, and a
king shall die on the field of battle." Those who heard
this prediction feared that he alluded to the eldest
son of Philip-Augustus, who had vowed to join the
Crusade against the Albigenses, but Dominic reas-
sured them, saying, "Fear not for the king of France;
it is another king who will soon lose his life in this
war." [1] Shortly after, Pedro of Aragon was slain at

---

[1] The Blessed Humbert's *Vie de St. Dominique*, n. 48.

Muret.

Dominic's fixed intention of founding a Religious Order, dedicated to the work of preaching, seeming likely to be perpetually frustrated by the duration and vicissitudes of the war, he instantly besought God to restore peace and order. To obtain his request, and hasten the triumph of the faith, he, moved by secret inspiration, instituted that form of prayer since then so universally practised throughout the Church under the name of *Rosary*. When the Archangel Gabriel was sent by God to announce to the Blessed Virgin the mystery of the Incarnation, he saluted her in these words, *"Hail, Mary, full of grace; the Lord is with thee; blessed art thou among women!"* [1] These words, most blessed of all that have fallen on mortal ears, are from age to age reechoed by Christian lips, and from the depths of this vale of tears they ever salute the Mother of Jesus in these words, *"Hail, Mary, full of grace."* From out the ranks of their most exalted leaders, the heavenly hierarchy selected him who should greet the lowly daughter of David with that glorious salutation; and now that she is throned far above celestial and angelic choirs, the human race, whose daughter and sifter she is, still waft to her that angel's greeting, *"Hail, Mary, full of grace."* As soon as she heard the Archangel's words, the Son of God was conceived in her chaste womb; and now, whenever mortal lips repeat the angelic salutation, the signal of her maternity, she thrills at the recollection of a moment

---

[1] St. Luke i. 28.

unparalleled in heaven and earth, and all eternity is partaker of her joy.

But though Christians were thus wont, from time immemorial, to raise their hearts to the Blessed Virgin, the salutation was used in a vague and general way; the faithful did not assemble together to address their cherished patroness, but each individual followed his own loving impulse. Dominic, knowing the efficacy of united prayer, thought it would be well to recite the Angelus in the same manner, so that the cry of an assembled multitude might the more readily mount to heaven. The brevity of the angel's words rendered it necessary that they should be often repeated, even as those reiterated acclamations with which a grateful people hails the presence of its sovereign. But as repetition may engender distractions, Dominic guarded against this, by arranging the Hail Maries in series, assigning to each, one of the chief mysteries of our redemption, which mysteries were for the Blessed Virgin a source of joy, sorrow, and triumph. In this way the faithful, while saluting their Queen and Mother, followed, in spirit, the principal events of her life, thus uniting prayer with meditation. In order the better to ensure the perpetuity and reverent observance of this devotion, Dominic established a Confraternity. His pious efforts were crowned by success; the devotion became most popular, and the faithful from age to age have never wavered in their attachment to it. The number of Confraternities has multiplied *ad infinitum*, and there is scarcely any Christian but possesses in the form of "Chaplet" some portion of the Rosary. Who does not remember having heard the grave voices of the peasants reciting the angelic salutation in the village churches? Who but has met processions of pilgrims telling their beads, and beguiling the weariness of the way by the repetition of Mary's name? Nothing attains perpetuity and universality but what is in mysterious accord with the wants and destinies of man. The rationalist smiles on beholding a string of people repeating the same word, but he who is illuminated by a higher light, knows that love has but one word, which, because ever on its lips, is never repeated.

The devotion of the Rosary, although interrupted in the fourteenth century by a terrible pestilence which ravaged Europe, was nevertheless revived in the next century by Alain de la Roche, a Dominican of Brittany; and in 1573, in order to commemorate the celebrated battle of Lepanto, in which the Turks were defeated during the pontificate of a Dominican Pope, on the very day when the Confraternities of the Rosary were holding public processions in Rome and throughout Christendom, Gregory XIII. instituted the feast, since then annually celebrated by the Church under the name of the *Feast of the Rosary*.

Such were the arms with which Dominic combated heresy and the evils of war; preaching, amid insult, controversy, patience, and voluntary poverty; a life of self-denial; a boundless charity; the gifts of miracles; and, lastly, the promotion of devotion to Our Lady by the institution of the Rosary. The ten years elapsing between the interview at Montpellier and the Lateran Council, were so uniform in their tenor, that contemporary historians have discerned but few actions to chronicle, in this humble, heroic, and constant exercise of the same virtues. The fear of being monotonous arrested their pen, for the history of a few days would be the history of entire years of Dominic's life. The uniformity of this great man's life, at such a stirring epoch, is the trait that distinguishes Dominic from Montfort. United by a sincere friendship and a common aim, their characters nevertheless as dissimilar as the knight's armour and the monk's habit. The sun of history illumes the cuirass of the warrior, revealing brilliant lights and deep shadows; hardly a ray falls on the garb of Dominic, but that, so pure and so holy, that the absence of a greater brilliancy is in itself a striking homage. Dominic is in obscurity because he has withdrawn from tumult and from bloodshed, because, faithful to his mission, he has opened his lips but to bless, his heart but to pray, and his hands but for deeds of mercy, and because virtue, when hidden from man, is invisible to all, save God.

Dominic was in his forty-sixth year when he began to reap the fruit of his long labours. In 1215 the gates of Toulouse were thrown open to him by the Crusaders; and Providence, who often assembles together the most diverse elements, sent him two men as the nucleus of the future Order of Friar Preachers. Both were citizens of Toulouse, of distinguished birth and remarkable character. The one, Pierre Cellani, a man of large fortune and distinguished virtue; the other, known to us only as Thomas, was noted for his eloquence and singular amiability. Prompted by the same holy inspiration, they simultaneously gave themselves to Dominic; and Pierre Cellani presented the latter with his own beautiful house, situated close to the Château of Narbonne, belonging to the Counts of Toulouse. There Dominic gathered together all his followers, numbering six, viz., Pierre Cellani, Thomas, and four others. It was but a very small band, and yet had cost ten years of apostolate, and forty-five years of a life wholly dedicated to the service of God. How little do they who act precipitately, or they who are disheartened by obstacles, know of the conditions attached to durability! Since that night at Toulouse, when, after the conversion of his heretical host, Dominic first conceived the idea of his future Order, time had showed itself inexorable to him. Left an orphan in a strange land, by the death of his friend and master, Azévédo; surrounded on every side by the sanguinary conflict of war; an object of inveterate hatred to the heretics, now embittered by opposition; he, seeing that the time and energy of the Catholics were devoted to another cause than that of the apostolate, beheld himself reduced to a state of hopeless solitude.

But God scatters the clouds; the Count of Toulouse, though destined to die at home, victorious and tranquil, is for a while rendered powerless by a battle as decisive as it was unforeseen. God grants His servant some months of peace, and the Order of Friar Preachers is founded in the very seat of heresy, and during the interval separating two stormy epochs.

The dress assigned to his companions was similar to that worn by himself, viz., a white woollen tunic, linen surplice, and cape and cowl of black wool. This was the garb of the Canons Regular, worn by him since his admission to the Chapter at Osma, and retained by himself and followers, until changed by the occurrence of a memorable event, which in due time we shall record. They also lived by rule; and their establishment took place with the co-operation, and by the authority, of Foulques, Bishop of Toulouse, that same generous Cistercian who from the commencement evinced such warm interest in the mutual project of Dominic and Azévédo. Not content with giving it merely the benefit of his patronage, we have, in the following, a proof of his generosity on their behalf, so signal as to merit the everlasting gratitude of the Order. "In the name of, our Lord Jesus Christ, be it known to all, now and henceforth, that we, Foulques, by the grace of God, humble servant of the See of Toulouse, desiring to extirpate heresy and banish vice, to teach men the rule of faith and mould them to virtue, institute, as preachers in our diocese, Brother Dominic and his companions, who, as barefooted religious, purpose preaching the gospel and pursuing the path of evangelic poverty. And because the labourer is worthy of his hire, and because it is forbidden to muzzle the ox that treadeth out the corn, also because he who preaches the gospel should live by the gospel, we desire that Brother Dominic and his companions, in sowing the word of truth in our diocese, may at the same time have their material wants supplied; therefore, with the consent of the Chapter of St. Etienne and that of all the clergy in our diocese, to them and to all such as, moved by zeal in the Lord's service and desirous of the salvation of souls, shall follow in their steps, we assign, in perpetuity, the sixth part of the tithes accruing to our parish churches, for the relief of their necessities, and in order that from time to time they may be enabled to rest from their labour. If, at the close of the year, any surplus remain, we enjoin that it be employed in the decoration of our parish churches, or for the relief of the poor, as may seem good to the Bishop. Seeing that a certain portion of the tithes should be consecrated to the poor, those are fitting recipients who embrace poverty for love of Jesus Christ, intending to benefit the world by their example and by the heavenly gift of wisdom; and as they minister to us in spiritual things, so in return must we, directly or indirectly, minister to them in temporal things. Given in the year of grace 1215,in the reign of Philip, king of France, and during the rule of Montfort, Count of Toulouse."[1]

This munificent deed did not stand alone; others came also to the help of the rising Order of Friar Preachers. "At this time," say historians, "Simon, Count de Montfort, combating the heretics with the *material sword*, and Brother Dominic combating them with the *sword of God's Word*, were united in intimate friendship." Montfort gave his friend Dominic the chateau and lands of Cassanct, in the diocese of Agen, having already confirmed several donations in favour of the convent of Prouille, the possessions of which he had greatly augmented. These were not

---

[1] Echard's *Ecrivains de l'Ordre des Prêcheurs*, vol. i. p. 12, note.

the sole proofs of the esteem and affection he evinced for Dominic, whom he entreated not only to baptize his daughter, betrothed during a brief time to the heir of Aragon, but also to bless the union of his eldest son, Count Amaury, with Beatrice, daughter of the Dauphine of Vienne.

In his later years we shall behold Dominic regret having accepted these temporal possessions, which he will renounce, bequeathing as sole patrimony to his children that Providence who supplies the daily needs of every zealous worker, and of whom it is written, "Cast thy care upon the Lord, and He shall sustain thee." [1]

---

[1] Psalm liv. 23.

CHAPTER VII.

Dominic's second journey to Rome—Innocent III.'s conditional approval of the Order of Friar Preachers—Meeting of St. Dominic and St. Francis of Assisi.

HAVING seen his idea thus far realised, Dominic allowed himself to hope for the approval of the Holy See. Therefore, taking advantage of the approaching Lateran Council, he set out for Rome in the autumn of the year 1215, accompanied by the Bishop of Toulouse. But before taking leave of his disciples, he, by one act, finally traced out for his Order one of the grand routes to be pursued by them. At that time, Alexander, a celebrated doctor, filled the chair of theology at Toulouse. While studying one morning at a very early hour, he was so oppressed by drowsiness that he fell into a deep sleep, during which he beheld seven stars appear, which, though small at first, gradually increased in size and brilliancy, until at last France and the whole world was illumined by their splendour. Awaking from this dream at dawn of day, he summoned the servants who were in the habit of carrying his books, and betook himself to his school. Just as he was entering, Dominic appeared, accompanied by his disciples, all wearing the white tunic and black cape of the Canons Regular. They said that they were Brothers, engaged in preaching the gospel to the inhabitants of the province of Toulouse, and that they ardently desired to listen to his teaching. Then Alexander knew that these were the seven stars just seen by him in his dream; and when staying, later on, at the court of the king of England, at a time when the Order of Friar Preachers had acquired great renown, he related in what manner the earliest members of that new Order had been enrolled among his pupils.

After confiding his disciples to the guard of prayer and study, Dominic proceeded to Rome. Twelve years had elapsed since Don Diégo and he had visited it for the first time, as pilgrims, and both as yet unconscious why from such a far distance they had been led by God to the feet of His Vicar. Now Dominic brings back to the Holy Father the fruit of his benediction; and although robbed by death of the companion of his former pilgrimage, he does not return alone. He was destined to form many illustrious friendships; and if Spain, the land of his birth, kept guard over the tomb of the friend and patron of Dominic's early years, France, the land of his adoption, had given him, in the person of Foulques, another protector and another friend. Although he had the happiness of finding Innocent III. still the occupant of the Papal throne, the Holy Father did not at once accede to Dominic's request. He had readily consented to take the convent of Prouille under the guardianship of the Holy See, and had issued letters to that effect, dated 8th October 1215; but the Holy

Father hesitated to give his approval to a new Order dedicated to preaching.

Historians allege two reasons for this repugnance. First, that preaching being an office transmitted by the Apostles to the Bishops, it seemed contrary to antiquity that it should be exercised by any other than the Episcopal order. True that the Bishops had for some time voluntarily abstained from the honour of announcing the Word of God, and that the fourth Lateran Council, recently held, had enjoined that the pulpits should be filled by Priests, capable of preaching in the Bishop's stead. Still, it was one thing for each individual Bishop to provide for instruction throughout his diocese by the appointment of vicars revocable at will, and another to confide to a particular Order the perpetual and universal function of preaching. Would not the latter virtually be the formation of an apostolic order within the Church, and could any other apostolic order exist besides that of the Episcopacy? Such was the question to which Dominic's zeal had given birth—a question this which Innocent III. could not at once resolve, as, notwithstanding the above-named reasons, much was to be said on the other side. The apostolate was decidedly languishing, and the increasing spread of heresy was due to the absence of skilled and zealous instruction. The councils held in Languedoc during the Albigensian war, had unanimously reminded the Bishops of this part of their duty. But Apostles are created by the grace of God, and not by the decrees of councils. On returning to their palaces, the Bishops

found in the administration of diocesan and state affairs, and in the almost irresistible force of
circumstances, an excuse for their religious inertia.
Neither was it an easy thing to find persons who
could instruct in their stead. One cannot say to a
Priest, "Be thou an Apostle!" The apostolic character
is the result of a particular course of life. Such was
common in the Early Church, because the whole
world having to be conquered, all minds pursued the
only course of action capable of attaining that end.
But since the Church has become the universal sovereign of nations, the pastoral office has superseded
the apostolic one, the aim being rather to preserve
than to extend the kingdom of Christ. Now, by a law
to which all created things are subject—where progress ends, death begins—the conservative regime,
though sufficing with the majority, is incapable of re-
straining certain ardent minds that escape from a
service that does not urge them onwards, as soldiers
weary when never led to face the foe. Such souls,
though isolated at first, rally together unobserved,
creating the excitement they need, until the day
when, deeming themselves sufficiently strong, they
teach the Church, by their sudden irruption, that the
human intellect is kept faithful in its allegiance to
truth only by dint of perpetual reconquest. . . . The
state of Europe had but too well revealed this law of
humanity to Innocent III. Ought he then to refuse
the succour so opportunely proffered, and resist the
Divine Spirit, who, besides raising up to His Church
many a worthy Bishop, now gave a band of Monks as
their co-operators? Still, there was a difficulty in the

way. The Lateran Council having decreed, that in order to avoid the confusion and inconvenience resulting from the multiplicity of Religious Orders, no new ones should be founded, how could he act in opposition to this solemn decision?

God, who vouchsafes to the Catholic Church an assistance, the perpetuity of which is one of the visible miracles of His wisdom, desiring only to prove Dominic by this final trial, now dissipated the Holy Father's anxiety. Sleeping one night in the palace of St. John Lateran, he dreamt he saw the basilica about to fall, and Dominic supporting the falling walls on his own shoulders. Warned by this inspiration, he sent for Dominic, whom he ordered to return to Languedoc, to select, in concert with his companions, that one of the ancient Rules which should appear to him most suited for the formation of the new militia with which he desired to enrich the Church. In this way the Lateran decree would be observed, and the seal and protection of antiquity given to the new undertaking.

While in Rome, another great joy awaited Dominic. He was not the only one elected by Providence to succour the Church in those critical times. Whilst the life-giving stream of God's Word welled forth from the pure and saintly depths of Dominic's heart, another man had been called of God to revive in His Church, amid the soul-destroying luxury of the age, the love and observance of poverty. This sublime lover of Jesus Christ was born in the town of Assisi, at the foot of the Umbrian hills, and was the son of a rich, but miserly, merchant. Having learnt French

in the interests of his father's business, they called
him Francis, although it was neither his baptismal
nor family name. Returning from Rome at the age of
twenty-four, he, often solicited by the Spirit of God,
was now wholly taken possession of by the same. Being led by his father into the presence of the Bishop
of Assisi in order that he might renounce all his family rights, the heroic young man, stripping himself of
all his clothes, laid them at the Bishop's feet, saying,
"Now I can say with more truth than ever, '*Our Father who art in heaven.*'" [1] A little later on, being
present at the Holy Sacrifice, he heard that part of
the Gospel read where Jesus Christ tells His Apostles to take nothing for their journey, neither staff,
nor scrip, nor bread, nor money, neither to have two
coats. On hearing these words, he was filled with an
inexpressible joy; he took off his shoes, cast aside his
staff, with horror threw away the little money he possessed, and during the remainder of his life wore no
other garment than an under one, a tunic, and a cord.
Even these appeared too great riches, and before his
death he had himself laid on the pavement in presence of his brethren, nude as in the day when, on his
final conversion, he placed his garments at the
Bishop's feet.

Whilst these events were occurring, Dominic, at
peril of his life, was evangelising Languedoc, and
crushing heresy by his apostolic labours. Unknown
to themselves, a wondrous harmony had been established between these two men, and the similarity of

---

[1] St. Bonaventure, *Vie de St. François*, chap. ii.

their career extended even to the events which followed their death. Dominic was the senior by two years; and having been trained in a more learned manner for his mission, was in due time joined by this young brother, who needed no universities to teach him the science of poverty and of love. Almost at the same instant that Dominic was laying the foundation of his Order at Notre-Dame-de-Prouille, at the foot of the Pyrenees, Francis was laying the foundation of his at Notre-Dame-des-Anges, at the foot of the Apennines. An ancient sanctuary of the Blessed Virgin, Mother of God, was the sweet and lowly corner-stone of both these edifices. Notre-Dame-de-Prouille was Dominic's cherished spot; whilst Notre-Dame-des-Anges was the one spot of ground for which Francis had reserved a place in the immensity of a heart detached from all things visible. Both had commenced their public life by a pilgrimage to Rome, whither they returned to solicit for their Orders the approbation of the Holy Father. At first Innocent III. refused their appeal, but was afterwards constrained by the same vision to give a verbal and conditional approval to both. As Francis, so Dominic, embraced within the flexible austerity of his Rule, men, women, and people of the world, making of three Orders one single power combating for Jesus Christ with the arms of nature and of grace; the only difference was, that while the first members of Dominic's order were women, those of St. Francis' were men. The same Sovereign Pontiff, Honorius III., confirmed their institutions by apostolic Bulls, and the same Pope, Gregory IX., canonised them both. Also the two greatest doctors of all ages arose from their ashes; St. Thomas from those of Dominic, and St. Bonaventure from those of Francis.

Yet these two men, whose destinies were so harmonious in the sight of heaven and earth, were strangers to one another, and although both were in Rome during the fourth Lateran Council, it does not appear that they ever heard of each other. One night when Dominic was praying, he beheld Jesus Christ filled with wrath against the world, and His Blessed Mother presenting to Him two men, in order to appease Him. He recognised himself as one, but did not know the other, whom he regarded so attentively that the face was ever present to him. On the morrow, in a church, we know not which, he beheld, in the dress of a mendicant, the face seen by him the preceding night, and running to the poor man, embraced him with holy effusion, uttering these words, "You are my companion; you will walk with me; let us keep together and none shall prevail against us." He then related his vision, and thus were their hearts blended in one.

The kiss of Dominic and Francis has been transmitted from generation to generation on the lips of their posterity. The two Orders are still united by the ties of early friendship; they are to be seen filling the same office in every part of the globe; their monasteries are erected in the same localities, and they beg at the same doors; and their blood shed in the cause of Jesus Christ has mingled a thousand times in the same glorious sacrifice; princes and princesses have donned their habit; they have peopled heaven with their saints; their virtue, influence, renown, and aims have ever been the same; and never has the breath of jealousy tarnished the purity of a friendship of six hundred years' duration. They have spread together throughout the world, even as two trees equal in age and strength joyously interlace their branches; they have won and shared the affections of nations, as twin-brothers rest on the bosom of the same mother; they have trod the same path to heaven, even as two precious perfumes mounting heavenwards by the same path.

Every year when the Feast of St. Dominic occurs, carriages are to be seen starting from the monastery of Sainte-Marie-sur-Minerve, where dwells the General of the Order of St, Dominic, in order to escort the General of the Franciscans from the monastery of Ara-Cœli. He arrives, accompanied by a large number of his brethren, and Dominicans and Franciscans proceed in parallel lines to the high altar of Santa Maria, when, after mutual salutations, the former take their place in the choir, the latter remaining at the altar to celebrate the office of their father's friend. Then, seated at the same table, they break the bread which for six hundred years has never failed them; and the repast ended, the chanters of both Orders sing in concert, in the midst of the Refectory, this anthem: "The seraphic Francis and the apostolic Dominic have given us Thy law, O Lord!"

This interchange of greetings, which takes place in the monastery of Ara-Cœli, has its counterpart throughout the world wherever a Dominican and Franciscan monastery are sufficiently near to permit the inhabitants interchanging the mutual sign of the holy and *hereditary* affection by which they are united.

CHAPTER VIII.

St. Dominic and his disciples meet at Notre-Dame-de-Prouille—Rule and Constitution of the Friar Preachers—Foundation of the Monastery of St. Romain in Toulouse.

DURING Dominic's absence, God had both blessed and multiplied his little flock; in lieu of the six disciples left by him in Pierre Cellani's house, in Toulouse, he now found fifteen or sixteen. After the first effusions of joy at re-union, Notre-Dame-de-Prouilie was appointed by Dominic as the meeting place where to deliberate, in conformity with the Pope's commands, as to the selection of their Rule. Until that time, in the spring of 1216, their community had only an indefinite and provisional form, as Dominic had devoted himself rather to action than to writing, after the manner of our Lord, who formed His Apostles for their mission, not by written Rules, but by word and by example. Now the hour had arrived when the Dominican family must receive its Rule, so that its mode of life might be defined and perpetuated. Already a father, Dominic must now become a legislator, and after giving birth to a generation of men like unto himself, he was now about to ensure their perpetuity, and arm them against the future, by that mysterious power which confers durability.

If the perpetuity of an earthly family be a *chef d'œuvre* of virtue and skill, if the foundation of empires demand human genius of the highest order, what must not be requisite to establish a society purely spiritual, not owing its existence to human affections, nor its defence to sword or shield? Ancient legislators, alarmed at their task, attributed a divine origin to their nations, and this by a lie but too apparent. Living in the Christian era, when the plenitude of reality had replaced the ruins of fiction, Dominic had no need to deceive. Ere venturing to trace a single law, he cast himself at the feet of God's Vicegerent, imploring that benediction which is the germ of a lasting posterity. Then withdrawing into solitude, and placing himself under the protection of the Virgin Mother, he ardently besought God to grant him a share of that Spirit to whom the Catholic Church is indebted for her lasting foundations.

St. Augustine and St. Benedict, born a century apart, were the founders of monastic life in the West, but neither had the end in view proposed by Dominic. St. Augustine, recently converted, retired with a few friends to a house at Tagaste, his native place, in order to devote himself to the study of divine things. Later on, when raised to the priesthood, he founded another monastery in Hippo, which, with its predecessor, was but a reminiscence of the famous Cenobitic institutions owing their origin to St. Anthony and St. Basil. Having succeeded the aged Valerius in the See of Hippo, although his views changed, he still retained his ardent love for community life. He opened his house to the clergy of Hippo, forming his co-operators into one single community. This episcopal monastery served as a model and starting point for the Canons Regular, as that of Tagaste had served as model to the religious known as the hermits of St. Augustine. As for St. Benedict, his work was still further removed from the end Dominic had in view, inasmuch as the former merely revived the purely monastic life, dividing it between the service of the choir and manual labour.

Compelled to select as ancestor one of these great men, Dominic's choice fell on St. Augustine. The reasons are easily discerned; for although the illustrious Bishop had no intention of founding an Apostolic Order, he had been apostle and doctor too; his life had been spent in preaching God's Word, and in defending it from the heretics of his day; and therefore his Rule seemed the most appropriate to the new Order of Friar Preachers. Moreover, it was a Rule not unfamiliar to Dominic during the many years spent by him in the Chapter of Osma, and was well adapted to his new Order. Also the Rule of St. Augustine possessed this advantage, that being a simple exposition of the fundamental duties of a religious life, it prescribed no settled form of government, no observance, save community of goods, prayer, frugality, the careful guard of the senses, mutual correction of faults, obedience to the monastic superior, and, above all, that chastity, the name and unction of which fills those pages, so admirable but so brief. In submitting himself to these prescriptions, Dominic accepted in reality nothing but the yoke of evangelic counsels; as to the rest, he was left unfettered by this

sketch, designed by a hand apparently less desirous
of creating a cloister than a city, within whose ancient ramparts the structure of the Friar Preachers
was to be erected.

One question presented itself, which was this:
should an Order destined to the apostolate adopt a
monastic life, or one resembling that led by the secular priesthood? There was no question of the three
vows of poverty, chastity, and obedience, without
which we can imagine no spiritual society existing,
any more than we can imagine a nation not subjected
to the poverty of taxation, the chastity of the mar-
riage-tie, and obedience to the same laws and
governors. But would the end in view be furthered
by the observance of such customs as the public reci-
tation of the Divine Office, perpetual abstinence from
meat, long fasts, silence, the chapter called "culpa,"
penances inflicted for non-observance of the Rule,
and manual labour? Would this rigorous discipline,
fitted to mould the solitary heart of the monk and
sanctify the leisure of his days, be compatible with
the heroic liberty of an apostle who has to take his
onward way, sowing on each hand the good seed of
the truth? Dominic thought so. It seemed to him
that by replacing manual labour by the study of divine things, by the mitigation of certain practices; by
the use of dispensations with regard to those Religious who were more strictly occupied in teaching
and preaching, it would be possible to reconcile apostolic action with monastic observance. Perhaps the
idea of separating them never entered Dominic's

mind; for the apostle is not only a man understanding and preaching God's Word, he is also a man whose whole being preaches Christianity, and whose very presence is in itself a manifestation of Jesus Christ. What so fit as the austerities of the cloister to impress on him the sacred stigmata of that resemblance? Dominic was nought else than an intimate union of the monk and the apostle. Study, prayer, preaching, fasting, sleeping on the ground, walking barefoot, performing penances, making proselytes; such being his daily life, who could better know all the affinity between the cloister and the apostolate?

The monastic traditions were therefore received at Prouille with some modifications, the first and most general being: "That each prelate should have power to dispense the brethren from the ordinary regulations whenever he should think fit, specially in those things which would hinder study, preaching, or the welfare of souls. Our Order having been originally and specially constituted for the purpose of preaching and for the salvation of souls, all our efforts must incessantly tend to promote the spiritual welfare of our neighbour."[1]

Therefore it was decreed that the Divine Office should be said in the church with brevity and succinctness, so that neither should the devotion of the brethren suffer, nor their studies be hindered; that when journeying, they should be exempted from fasting, save during Advent; on certain Vigils; and on the Fridays throughout the year; that they might eat

---

[1] *Constitutions de l'Ordre des Frères Prêcheurs*, Prologue, n. 3.

meat out of their own monasteries; that absolute silence should not be enjoined; that strangers, women
excepted, would be admitted within the monasteries;
that a certain number of students should be sent to
the most celebrated universities; that they should
take scientific degrees, and should hold schools. Regulations these which, without destroying the
monastic character of the Friar Preacher, raised him
to the rank of an apostolic labourer.

As regarded the administration, each monastery
was to be governed by a Prior; each province, consisting of a certain number of monasteries, to be
governed by a Prior Provincial, and the whole Order
by one Chief, since known as the Master-General. As
all the degrees of this hierarchy were to be confirmed
by the superior power, emanating in the first place
from the Sovereign Pontiff, and were to be elected by
their inferiors, a spirit of fraternity would thus be en-
sured. A twofold sign would be visible on the brow of
all in office—the election of his brethren and the approval of the superior power. The monks would elect
their own Prior; the province, represented by the Priors and one deputy from each monastery, would elect
the Provincial; the whole Order, represented by the
Provincial and two deputies from each province,
would elect the Master-General; whilst, on the other
hand, the General would confirm the choice of the
Prior Provincial, the Prior Provincial that of the
Prior of the monastery. All these functions, save the
highest, were temporary, so that to stability should
be associated the emulation attendant on change.
Chapters-General, held at frequent intervals, would

counter-balance the power of the General, and Provincial Chapters that of the Prior Provincial. A council was assigned the Prior of the monastery to assist him in the most important duties of his office. The wisdom of this form of government has been proved by experience. By it the Order of Friar Preachers has fully accomplished its destiny, preserved alike from license and from oppression. A sincere respect for authority, added to a certain frankness and naturalness, reveals at first glance the Christian freed from fear by love. The majority of the Religious Orders have been subjected to reforms dividing them into several offshoots; that of the Friar Preachers has retained its unity amid the vicissitudes of six hundred years, extending its vigorous branches throughout the whole world, without a single one being separated from the parent stock.

Another question remained: how should the Order subsist? From the first day of his own apostolate, Dominic had trusted to the Divine bounty, living on daily alms, handing over to Prouille all save just enough to provide for his immediate wants. Not until he had witnessed the growth of his spiritual family, did Dominic accept from Foulques the sixth of the tithes of the Toulouse diocese, and from Montfort the estate of Cassanel. But all his affection and all his heart was given to poverty. He discerned the wounds inflicted on the Church by opulence too clearly to desire for his own Order other riches than those of virtue. Nevertheless the assembly at Prouille deferred to a future day the statute concerning mendicity. Dominic doubtless feared that Rome

might oppose so daring a thought, and therefore preferred reserving its execution for a less critical time.

Such were the fundamental laws laid down by the
founders of the Dominican Order. In comparing
them with those of the Canons Regular of Prémontré,
despite the diversity of aim, one remarks a likeness
which proves that Dominic had carefully studied the
work of St. Norbert. Probably he had done so while
at Osma; and the reform of Prémontré may have
served as a model for the reform of the Chapter of
Osma.

Foulques, ever occupied in furthering Dominic's
designs, gave him three churches; one at Toulouse,
under the invocation of St. Romain the Martyr; the
second at Pamiers; and the third situated between
Sorèze and Puy-Laurens, and known by the name of
Notre-Dame-de-Lescure. Although it was intended
to erect a Dominican monastery in each of these
spots, none was ever built at Notre-Dame-de-Lescure, nor at Pamiers, until the year 1269. As we have
already stated, the heretical city of Toulouse was the
first to witness the erection of a Dominican monastery; for although the monks had dwelt together
since the previous year, their house resembled a
monastery in nothing save the life of its inmates
therefore it was necessary to erect a suitable building, which was speedily reared in the form of a
modest cloister attached to the Church of St. Romain.
A cloister is a court surrounded by a portico; in the
midst of which court, according to ancient traditions,
should be a well, symbol of that living water *springing up to eternal life.* Beneath the stones of the

portico or covered walk were the tombs; funereal in-
scriptions were graven on the walls; and in the
arched vaulting of the portico were painted the acts
of the saints belonging to the Order, or to the monastery. This spot was sacred; the very monks paced
there in silence, their minds filled with the thoughts
of death, or the memory of their predecessors. The
sacristy, refectory, and large general rooms were
ranged round this solemn gallery, which communi-
cated with the church by two doors, the one leading
to the choir, the other into the nave. A flight of stairs
led to the upper stories, constructed above the gallery and on the same plan. Four windows, opening
at the four corners of the corridors, supplied them
with abundant light, and four lamps illumined them
at night. Along these spacious and lofty corridors,
whose sole luxury consisted in their cleanliness, the
charmed eye discerned a symmetrical line of doors on
the right hand and on the left. In the intervening
spaces were suspended a thousand simple souvenirs
of heaven and earth, such as old pictures, maps,
plans of cities and ancient castles, and a table of the
monasteries of the Order. At the sound of a clock
every door gently opened. Hoary and serene-looking
old men, men of precocious maturity, young men in
whom penance and youth had formed a type of
beauty unknown to the world, every age of life here
appeared wearing the same garb. The cell of the Ce-
nobites was poor, but sufficiently large to contain a
straw or horse-hair bed, a table and two chairs; a crucifix and a few religious pictures being the sole

ornaments. From this tomb, where he spent his mortal life, the monk passed to that tomb which precedes immortality. Even there he was not separated from his living and departed brethren. He was laid, in monastic garb, beneath the pavement of the choir; his dust mingled with that of his predecessors; whilst the praises of the Lord, sung by his contemporaries and successors in the choir, re-echoed around his tomb. Amiable and holy dwellings! Earth has witnessed the erection of splendid palaces, sublime sepulchres, temples all but divine; yet never have human skill and love created aught so perfect as the cloister.

That of St. Romain was ready by the end of August in the year 1216. In structure it was unpretending; the cells were six feet broad and not quite so long; the partitions were not the height of a man, so that the brothers, while occupied in their respective duties, were at the same time partly in each others' presence. All the furniture was very poor. The Order retained this monastery only until 1232, when the Dominicans of Toulouse removed to a larger house and church, of which they were deprived by the French Revolution, and the magnificent ruins of which now serve as shops and barracks.

CHAPTER IX.

Dominic's third journey to Rome—Confirmation of the Order of Friar Preacher by Pope Honorius III.

WHILST the monastery of St. Romain was rapidly progressing under the eyes of Dominic, an unforeseen occurrence saddened the heart of the holy Patriarch. Innocent III. died at Perouse on the 10th July, and two days after, Cardinal Conti, of the ancient race of the Sabelli, was, by a hasty election, raised to the pontifical throne under the name of Honorius III. Death had thus deprived the Dominicans of a faithful protector, and exposed them to the uncertainties attendant on a new regime. Innocent III. belonged to that family of rare men whom Providence had given as friends and protectors to Dominic; he was of kindred blood with Azévédo, Foulques, and Montfort, that generous constellation of which the stars were being quenched one by one. Azévédo was the first to depart, leaving his heroic designs uncompleted; and now that Dominic had succeeded in furthering their execution under the auspices of Innocent III., this great Pontiff disappeared before completing his promised work. This trial was but of short duration. A third time Dominic crossed the Alps, and, in spite of the embarrassments attendant

on a new administration, at once obtained the reward due to his protracted labours. On December 22,
1216, his Order was solemnly confirmed by two
Bulls, as follows:—

"Honorius, Bishop, servant of the servants of God,
to his dear son Dominic, Prior of St. Remain of Toulouse, and to the professed brethren, present and
future, health and apostolic benediction. It behoves
that those professing the religious life should be
placed under apostolic protection, lest they should be
turned aside from their aim by rash attacks, or,
which God forbid, their religious life be imperilled.
Therefore, dear sons in the Lord, we readily accede
to your just demands and take under the protection
of the blessed Apostle Peter, and under our own, the
church of St. Romain of Toulouse, in the which you
have dedicated yourself to the divine service. We decree, first, that the canonical Order established in
this church, according to God's will and the rule of
St. Augustine, be perpetually and inviolably observed there; moreover, that the possessions justly
acquired by the said church, or eventually accruing
to her by pontifical concession, the alms of the faithful, or in any other legitimate way, remain
irrevocably in your hands and in those of your successors; We also deem it well to name the following
possessions, viz., the church of St. Romain and its dependencies, the church of Prouille and its
dependencies, the estate of Cassanel, the church of
Notre-Dame-de-Lescure with all its dependencies,
the hospital of Toulouse called Arnaud-Bérard and
its dependencies, the church of the Sainte-Trinité of

Lohens with its dependencies, and the tithes which our venerable brother Foulques, Bishop of Toulouse, in his pious and thoughtful generosity, has, with the consent of his Chapter, ceded to you. That no one presume to demand tithes on the lands cultivated by you, or at your own expense, or on the produce of your cattle. We permit your receiving and retaining, without fear of hindrance, clerics and laics desirous of quitting the world, provided they are bound by no other ties. We forbid your Religious, after their profession, to quit their Order without their Prior's permission, unless it be to embrace a severer Rule, and we likewise forbid any one to admit such without your consent. You will provide for the services of the parish churches belonging to you by presenting to the Bishop of the diocese Priests worthy of being appointed to the cure of souls, and who will be responsible to him, in things spiritual, and to you, in things temporal. We forbid that your church be subjected to any new conditions; we forbid that either it or you should be laid under an interdict or excommunicated, unless for a reasonable and manifest cause. In case of a general interdict, you may celebrate the Divine Office in a low voice, without bells, and with closed doors, after such as are excommunicated and under the interdict have quitted the church. Chrism, holy oil, consecration of altars or basilicas, ordination of your clerics, shall be obtained from the bishop of the diocese, provided that he be Catholic and in the grace and communion of the Holy See, and that he consent to give you the above without any unjust conditions; in the contrary case, you shall apply to any

Catholic bishop you may please to select, provided he
be in the grace and communion of the Holy See, and
he shall comply with your requests in virtue of our
authority. We grant you the right of sepulture in
your church; and forbid any opposition to the pious
and last wishes of such as desire to be interred there,
unless they are excommunicates or under an interdict, and provided that the right of sepulture
attaching to other churches be not interfered with.
At your decease and that of your successors in the
office of Prior, let no one take possession of the office
by ruse or violence, but he who has been duly elected
by all, or by the majority of the brethren, according
to God and the Rule of St. Augustine. We also ratify
the privileges, immunities, and reasonable customs
introduced of old and still existing in your church,
and desire that they may be observed inviolate. Let
none disturb the peace of this church; seize or retain,
diminish or meddle, with its possessions; but, saving
by apostolate authority or the canonical decision of
the diocesan, let such possessions remain intact, for
the use and support of those to whom they have been
conceded. If any person, ecclesiastical or secular,
cognisant of the above, dare to infringe this Order,
and on being warned a second and third time refuse
to give satisfaction, let him be deprived of all power
and honour, and let him know that he has rendered
himself guilty in the sight of God; let him be cut off
from the communion of the Body and Blood of our
Lord and Saviour Jesus Christ, and at the final judgment may he suffer severe punishment. On the other
hand, may the blessing of our Lord Jesus Christ be

upon all those who respect the rights of this church, and may here below receive the reward of their good deeds and an eternal recompense from the Sovereign Judge. Amen."[1]

The second Bull, brief as prophetic, runs thus:— "Honorius, servant of the servants of God, to the dear son Dominic, Prior of St. Romain of Toulouse, and to the professed brethren, health and apostolic benediction. We, considering that the Religious of your Order should be the *champions of the faith and the true luminaries of the world,* confirm your Order, with all its lands and possessions, present and future, and take beneath our shield and protection the Order itself, together with all its possessions and privileges."[2]

These two Bulls were issued at St. Sabine on the same day. The first bears not only the signature of Honorius, but the signatures of eighteen Cardinals also. Still, however favourable its terms, Dominic's wish was not fully granted; for he desired that the name of his Order might be a perpetual sign of the aim he had set before him in its institution. From the commencement of his apostolate he delighted in the name of *Preacher,* and by a deed of homage, at the signing of which he was present, on 21st June 1211, it is noticeable that he made use of a seal on which are graven these words, *"Seal of Brother Dominic, Friar."* When in Rome during the Lateran

---

[1] *Bulls of the Order of the Friars Preachers,* p. 2.

[2] Ibid., p. 4.

Council, says the Blessed Jourdain de Saxe, he proposed obtaining from the Pope an Order of Religious
filling the office and bearing the name of Preachers.
A remarkable fact occurred at this time. Innocent
III. having just encouraged Dominic by a verbal approval, and being under the necessity of writing to
him, called his secretary, saying, "Write such and
such things to Brother Dominic and his companions;"
then, after a moment's delay, continued, "Do not
write that, but say: 'To Brother Dominic and to those
who preach the gospel with him in the province of
Toulouse;' " then, stopping once more, he added, "To
Master Dominic and to the Friar Preachers."[1] Notwithstanding this, Honorius abstained from giving
the new Order any name in the Bulls issued by him.
It was doubtless to make reparation for this silence,
that a month later, on the 20th January 1217, he dic-
tated the following letter:—"Honorius, Bishop,
servant of the servants of God, to his dear sons the
Prior and the Religious of St. Romain, *Preachers* in
the province of Toulouse, health and apostolic Benediction. We render due thanks to the Author of Grace
for all the gifts He has conferred upon you, and in
which we hope to see you persevere even unto the
end. Consumed by the fire of charity, you shed
around you a sweet odour, rejoicing the hearts of
such as are whole, and restoring those who are sick.
As skilled physicians, you offer them spiritual man-
drakes preserving them from sterility, that is, the

---

[1]   Etienne de Salanhac, *Des Quaire Choses en quoi Dieu a
honoré l'Ordre des Frères Prêcheurs.*

seed of the Word fertilised by fervent eloquence. Faithful servants, the talent intrusted to you has fructified within your hands, and you will restore it to the Lord with increase. Invincible and strong in Christ, girt with the shield of faith and the helmet of salvation, you fear not those who can kill the body; courageously wielding against the enemies of the faith, that Word of God, sharper than any two-edged sword, and hating your lives in this world that you may save them in that which is to come. But as only the end crowns the work, and only he who perseveres shall be saved, we pray and exhort you seriously, by these apostolic letters, by your charity, and for the remission of your sins, to fortify yourselves yet more and more in the Lord, preaching the gospel in season and out of season, thus fully accomplishing the work of *evangelists.* If you endure tribulation for the Word's sake, bear it not only with equanimity, but, with the Apostle, glory and rejoice that ye are deemed worthy to suffer shame for the name of Jesus. For these light afflictions, which are but for a moment, work out an exceeding weight of glory, to which the sufferings of this present time are not worthy to be compared. We also beseech you, whom we regard with peculiar affection as our much loved sons, to intercede for us with God in your prayers, that so He may perchance vouchsafe to your petitions that which our own merits cannot obtain."

Thus were the office and name of Friar Preachers ascribed to the Dominicans by the Sovereign Pontiff. The three acts just cited show a remarkable gradation. In the first Bull, deliberated on in Consistory

and signed by the Cardinals, there is no question
whatever regarding the intention of the Order, which
is simply mentioned as a canonical Order under the
Rule of St. Augustine. The second Bull is briefer and
more concise, and names Dominic's spiritual children
champions of the faith, true lights of the world. The
last Bull *openly* styles them *Preachers*, praises them
for their past apostolic labours, and encourages them
with regard to the future. Historians have been puz-
zled as to the motives for this course of action, and
especially so as to the Sovereign Pontiff's reasons for
issuing two Bulls on the same subject, and on the
same day. They have conjectured that probably the
first was destined to be kept in the archives of the
Order, and the second to be used as a kind of daily
passport. But why should an Order sanctioned by
the Holy See need to present a Bull to all comers? Is
not its very existence a proof of its authenticity? And
in case of opposition, is it not clear that the important
document is the one defining its rights and privileges, and not the one, consisting of a few lines, in
which the question of its canonical status is left untouched? The progressive recognition of the Order of
Friar Preachers sets us on another track, and it
seems to us probable that at the pontifical court
there was some opposition to the establishment of an
apostolic Order, and that this was the cause of the
absolute silence observed in the first Bull regarding
the aims of the newly authorised Order; but that the
Sovereign Pontiff, yielding to divine inspiration and
to Dominic's urgency, signed a declaration on the

same day, stating the special motive by which Dominic was led; and a month later deemed it well to express himself openly and without reserve. On the 7th February Honorius ratified his first Bull by a Brief, forbidding the Friar Preachers to quit their Order save for a more austere one.

Having obtained his wish, Dominic must have been impatient to return to his spiritual children; but Lent was at hand and retained him in Rome, where he seized the opportunity thus afforded of commencing his ministrations in the very capital of Christendom. His success was great. He expounded St. Paul's Epistles to a numerous audience in the Vatican, thus proving that, apart from his controversies with the heretics, he followed in his teaching the method adopted by the Fathers, viz., the expounding Scripture to the people, not by detached portions, but in regular order, so that history, dogma, and morality were blended together, the main object of his eloquence being to impart instruction. The pulpit is a school of popular theology, and from the lips of the priest initiated in divine science the streams of eternal life, mingled with the traditions of the past and the hopes of the future, should flow to water the world. As this stream ebbs and flows, so does faith wax or wane. Elected by God to revive the apostolic office within the Church, Dominic had doubtless considered what was the best way of handling the Scriptures, and judging by his first essay in Rome, when in the prime of his maturity, we must conclude that he gave the preference to a continuous exposition of Holy Writ. A noteworthy fact attests the

success of his teaching. The Pope, desirous to secure
to the Roman people and the members of his court a
continuance of such instruction, made the office perpetual, and gave to the one filling it, the title of
Master of the Sacred Palace. Dominic was the first
to be invested with this office, which his descendants
have honourably filled until the present day. Its
privileges and duties have increased with time.
From preacher and doctor holding a spiritual school
in the Vatican, the Master of the Sacred Palace has
become theologian to the Pope, universal censor of
books printed at or brought into Rome, the only one
having power to confer the degree of Doctor in the
Roman University, and the elector of such as preach
before the Holy Father during the sacred seasons,—
functions to which are allied many honourable privileges, the heritage of which has been justly and
inviolably transmitted from Dominican to Dominican.

During the time that the holy Patriarch was becoming known in Rome by his preaching, he was also
a frequent guest of Cardinal Ugolino, Bishop of Ostia, and a member of the noble house of Conti. The
venerable Ugolino had worn the purple for twenty
years, and was at that period sixty-three years of age.
He was the friend of St. Francis of Assisi, who had
often predicted that Ugolino would one day wear the
tiara, and who often addressed him in his letters
thus: "To the very Reverend Father and Lord Ugolino, future Universal Bishop and Father." Despite
his years, Ugolino felt drawn to Dominic, as he had
been to Francis, to both of whom his still young heart

was capable of extending the same loving friendship. It is the privilege of certain souls to be susceptible of loving impulses even to their latest hour. So it was Dominic's privilege never to lose one friend without gaining another. God willed that the venerable Cardinal, destined to die Pope at the age of nearly a hundred, should render the last honours to Dominic, celebrate his funeral, and cherish his memory with pious affection, and, with the infallibility appertaining to his office, inscribe his name on the roll of the Saints. This was not the sole result of this illustrious friendship.

Among the members of the Cardinal's household was a young Italian named Giugliolmo de Montferrat, who had come to spend Easter at Rome, and on whom the appearance and discourses of Dominic made so deep an impression as to inspire him with the resolution described as follows:—"About sixteen years ago, I came to spend Lent in Rome, and the present Pope, then Bishop of Ostia, received me into his house. At that epoch, Dominic, the founder and first Master of the Order of Preachers, being at the Papal Court, often visited the Lord Bishop of Ostia, so that I became acquainted with him, and, taking pleasure in his conversation, began to love him. We often discoursed of the things appertaining to our common salvation; and it seemed to me that though I had frequently conversed with many holy men, never had I seen one who excelled him, nor any who appeared animated with such zeal for the salvation of men. The same year I went to Paris to study theology, because I had arranged that after two years spent in study, I would, as soon as Brother Dominic had made the final arrangements regarding his Order, accompany him, and labour with him for the conversion of the Persians and those dwelling in the northern countries."[1] Thus did Dominic gain the heart of the old man and that of the youth; and although his Order was scarcely established, he already meditated going in person to open to it the gates of the North and of the East. Fettered by European civilisation, his heart yearned to those nations on whom the light of Christianity had not yet dawned, among whom he ardently desired to end his days and seal his labours by his own blood.

He was encouraged in these ardent desires by a vision. One day that he was in St. Peter's, praying for the preservation and extension of his Order, St. Peter and St. Paul appeared, the former presenting him with a staff and the latter with a book, and a voice was heard saying to him, "Go and preach, for thereto have I chosen thee."[2] At the same moment he beheld his disciples, two by two, spreading throughout the whole world on their mission of evangelisation. From that day the Epistles of St. Paul and the Gospel of St. Matthew were his constant companions, and he was never seen abroad without a staff in his hand.

---

[1] *Actes de Bologne*, second deposition.
[2] Le B. Humbert, *Vie de St. Dominique*, n. 26.

CHAPTER X.

Re-union of the Friar Preachers at Notre-Dame-de-Prouille, and their dispersion through Europe.

ON LEAVING Rome after Easter in the year 1218, Dominic hastened to join his brethren. They were sixteen in number, eight Frenchmen, seven Spaniards, and one Englishman.

The Frenchmen were Guillaume Claret, Matthieu de France, Bertrand de Garrigue, Thomas, Pierre Cellani, Etienne de Metz, Noël de Prouille, and Odéric de Normandie. History has preserved their names and also a few of their distinguishing traits.

Guillaume Claret was a native of Pamiers, and one of the earliest of Dominic's companions. The Bishop of Osma, on quitting France, had intrusted him with the temporal administration of the Languedoc mission; and it is said that after being a member of the Order for twenty years, he joined the Cistercians at the Abbey of Bolbonne, and even wished to transfer the convent of Prouille there.

Matthieu de France had passed his youth in the schools in Paris, and had been appointed by Count Montfort to fill the office of Prior in the college of canons, at Saint-Vincent-de-Castres. While there, he met Dominic, and, after witnessing his ecstasy, devoted himself entirely to his service. He was the founder of the celebrated monastery of St. Jacques in Paris, and was buried in the choir of the church, at the foot of the stall which he had occupied as Prior of that monastery.

Bertrand de Garrigue, named after his birthplace, a little town near Alais in Languedoc, was a man of wonderful austerity. Dominic advised him, on one occasion, to weep less for his own sins and more for those of other men, and intrusted the government of St. Romain to Bertrand during his last journey to Italy. Bertrand died in 1230, and was buried at Orange, in a convent where many miracles were wrought by his relics, which in 1427 were removed, by command of Pope Martin V., to the monastery of Friar Preachers in the same town.

Thomas was a distinguished inhabitant of Toulouse, styled by Jourdain de Saxe a man full of grace and eloquence.[1] He and his fellow-citizen, Pierre Cellani, became Dominic's disciples on the same day.

Pierre Cellani, young, wealthy, and honourable, of noble birth and nobler heart, not only gave himself, but also his house to Dominic. He founded the monastery of Limoges, and was much venerated through the whole of his career. After filling the office of Grand Inquisitor, to which post he had been appointed by Gregory IX. during most troublous times, he died in the year 1259.

Etienne de Metz resided with Dominic at Carcassonne from the year 1213; he founded the monastery at Metz, hence his historical surname.

---

[1] *Vie de St. Dominique*, chap. 1.

Nothing particular is known regarding Noël de Prouille.

Odéric de Normandie was not a priest, but the first lay brother of the Order.

Such was the French element of the Dominican family at this time. Though few in number, their action was so rapid and extended, that one may well designate France as the mine and crucible whence issued the Friar Preachers. The daughters of France were also the first members of Notre-Dame-de-Prouille, that cradle of his Order. Saint-Romain-de-Toulouse owed its birth to two Frenchmen; and later on we shall see Matthew of Paris founding St. Jacques in Paris, and another Frenchman, whose name we know not, founding St. Nicolas in Bologna.

In studying the territorial position, history, and genius of France, we easily discern the part God predestined her to play in the formation of the Apostolic Order. If she has been termed a nation of soldiers, she is also a nation of missionaries, for her very sword proselytises. None has contributed more to the spread of Christ's kingdom in the West; and since the time of the Crusades her name in the Eastern tongues is synonymous with that of Christianity. At her baptism she received in equal measure the gift of faith and love, and her wonderful position and character threw open to her all the continents of the world. France is a vessel whose port is Europe, and whose anchors are cast in every sea. Need we wonder that God selected her to be, in Dominic's hand, the chief instrument of an Order whose action was destined to be universal? Spain was not wanting in fealty to the great man to whom she had given birth, and though engrossed in her patient and glorious struggle with the ancient rulers of her soil, she had sent more than one soldier to the spiritual army of her son. They were these: Dominic de Segovia. Suéro Gomez, the Blessed Mannès, Miguel de Fabra, Miguel de Uséro, Pedro de Madrid, and Juan de Navarre.

Dominic de Segovia was one of the earliest companions of the apostle of Languedoc. Jourdain de Saxe speaks of him as a man of *profound humility*, of little learning, but of great virtue.[1] It is related of him that a shameless woman having resolved to test his sanctity, he placed himself between burning brands, saying to the temptress, "If it be true that you love me, now is your time."[2]

Suéro Gomez was one of the leading nobles at the court of Sancho I., king of Portugal. The report of the Albigensian Crusade had attracted him to Languedoc, where he rendered chivalrous service to the Catholic cause. But God touched his heart, and recognising the superiority of that other army, he forsook all to preach Christ Jesus by word and by deed. He founded the monastery of Santarem on the Tagus, a few leagues from Lisbon; received many marks of confidence from King Alphonso II., and died in 1233. Many historians have given him the name of Saint.

The Blessed Mannès was Dominic's brother, but it

---

[1] Vie de St. Dominique, chap. i.
[2] Ibid.

is not known when or where he joined the Order. He died about the year 1230, and was buried in the ancestral tomb at Gumiel d'Izan.

Miguel de Fabra was the first reader or professor of theology pertaining to the Order. He taught in the monastery in Paris, was confessor and preacher to James, king of Aragon, and founded the Spanish monasteries in Majorca and Valencia. Ancient writers laud his apostolic zeal, the services rendered by him during the war with the Moors; his assiduity in prayer and meditation, and his miracles. His remains were deposited at first in the general burying-place of Friar Preachers in Valencia; but the Prior having been, warned by a prodigy to remove them to a more honourable spot, deposited them with great pomp in the conventual chapel of St. Peter the Martyr.

Nothing remarkable has been handed down to us by tradition respecting Miguel de Uséro and Pedro de Madrid.

Jean de Navarre was born at Saint-Jean-Pied-de-Port. He received the Dominican habit on the Feast of St. Augustine, 28th of August 1216, and is the only one of Dominic's early companions who served as witness during the process of his canonisation, and from his deposition we learn that they frequently travelled together.

As though each maritime nation must yield its tribute, England, in the person of Laurence, mingled one drop of her blood with that of France and Spain, in the first generation of the Dominican dynasty.

The joy experienced on Dominic's arrival was

equalled by the astonishment felt on learning his determination to disperse his flock at once. Every one had felt convinced that he would retain it for a long period within the saintly and studious shade of the cloister, instead of apparently destroying the unity of a body already so feeble. What could be expected from a few men scattered over Europe while their Order was yet unknown? The Archbishop of Narbonne, the Bishop of Toulouse, the Count of Montfort, and all interested in the new undertaking, entreated Dominic not to endanger its success by such a course of action. He, calm and immovable in his resolve, replied, "My lords and fathers, do not oppose me, for I well know what I am about."[1] He thought of the vision in St. Peter's and heard the two Apostles saying, "Go and preach." He had received another warning regarding the speedy fall of the Count of Montfort. He beheld in a dream a lofty tree covering the earth with its branches and giving shelter to the birds, when suddenly an unexpected stroke felled it to the ground, and scattered all that had fled to it for shelter. When such mysterious presages are from God, He affords a clue to their meaning. Dominic understood that Montfort was the tree, the fall of which would overthrow the hopes of the Catholics, and he knew that it would be unwise to build upon a tomb. In addition to these revelations, a keen insight into human character made him withstand the counsel given him by his friends. He believed that the apostle is formed rather by action than by contemplation,

---

[1] *Actes de Bologne*, deposition of Jean de Navarre, n. 2.

and that the surest way to recruit his Order was to plant it fearlessly amid the agitations to which the human intellect is exposed. He imparted this conviction to his disciples in words as striking as true: "Seed germinates when sown, and decays when accumulated."[1]

At this epoch three cities ruled in Europe—Rome, Paris, and Bologna: Rome by its Pontiff, and Paris and Bologna by their universities, whither the youth of all nations resorted. Dominic selected these three cities as the headquarters of his Order, members of which were to be instantly dispatched to each place. He could not forget his native land, although it had not yet taken part in the general European movement, neither could he desert Languedoc, which had received the first-fruits of his labours. We see, then, what a task he had undertaken, and the means with which he intended to accomplish it. He deemed sixteen men sufficient for Prouille, Toulouse, Rome, Paris, Bologna, and Spain. He did not stop there, but, as we have already seen, aspired to convert the nations of the East, having already let his beard grow after the Oriental manner, so that he might be ready to start with the first favourable wind. The same forethought prompted him to desire his brethren to elect canonically one of their number to replace him at his departure. Having arranged everything in his own mind, and enjoyed for a time the happiness of living with his children, he convoked them to the monastery of Prouille for the approaching Feast of

---

[1] Constantin d'Orviéto, n. 21; le B. Humbert, n. 26.

the Assumption. Among the numerous multitude
that thronged the church of Prouille on that day,
while some were attracted by the ancient sanctity of
the spot and others by curiosity, the Prelates,
Knights, and Simon, Count of Montfort, were drawn
thither by feelings of piety and affection. At that altar, which had so often witnessed his secret tears,
Dominic offered the Holy Sacrifice, received the solemn vows of his Religious, who until then were only
bound by a sentiment of fidelity, or by simple vows,
and having ended his address to them, turned to the
people, saying, "For many years I have exhorted you
tenderly; preaching, praying, and weeping, but all to
no purpose. The Spanish proverb says, 'Where ben-
edictions avail not, the rod may be effectual.' We
shall now stir up the Princes and Prelates, who will,
alas! arm nations and kingdoms to march against
this territory; and many will perish by the sword;
lands will be ravaged, walls overthrown, you will be
reduced to servitude, and thus will the rod avail
where benediction and gentleness were in vain." [1]
These farewells, addressed by Dominic to the un-
grateful country which had been for twelve years the
scene of his arduous labours, sound as expostulations
addressed to those who would one day traduce his
name. They clearly show us the character of that
apostolate, which consisted of *gentleness, exhorta-
tions, prayers, and tears.* The prophetic menace

---

[1] *Manuscrit de Prouille*, Records of the Monastery of Toulouse, by Père Percin, p. 20, n. 47.

recalls our Lord's well-known lamentation over Jerusalem: "If thou also hadst known, and that in this thy day, the things that are to thy peace; but now they are hidden from thine eyes. For the day shall come upon thee, and thy enemies shall cast a trench about thee, and compass thee round, and straiten thee on every side, and beat thee flat upon the ground, and thy children who are in thee, and they shall not leave in thee one stone upon another, because thou hast not known the time of thy visitation."[1] Dominic does not say that he will stir up the Princes and Prelates, but merging his own personality in that of Christendom, makes use of words denoting, not individual, but collective action: *"Against you we shall stir up princes and prelates."* Standing aloof from all that was wrought by justice and the sword, Dominic, lamenting over the coming woes, goes forth guiltless of human blood. He quits France, and in so doing, leaves the scene of conflict and the tumult of affairs. He is about to found monasteries in Italy, France, and Spain; and, staff in hand and wallet on back, will dedicate to this peaceful work the remainder of a life already exhausted by self-sacrifice.

The public ceremony ended, Dominic made known to his Friars his intentions regarding their future destination. Guillaume Claret and Noel de Prouille were to remain at the monastery of Notre-Dame-de-Prouille; Thomas and Pierre Cellani, at Toulouse; Dominic de Segovia, Suéro Gomez, Miguel de Uzéro, and Pedro de Madrid were allotted to Spain. Paris

---

[1] St. Luke xix. 42-44.

was to receive the three Frenchmen, Matthieu de France, Bertrand de Garrigue, and Odéric de Normandie; also the Spaniards, consisting of the Blessed Mannès, Miguel de Fabra and Juan de Navarre, and the Englishman Laurence, Dominic reserving only Etienne de Metz as coadjutor in the foundation of the monasteries of Bologna and Rome. Before separating, the Friars elected Matthew de France as Abbot, that is to say, as Superior-General of the Order, under the supreme authority of Dominic. This title, somewhat suggestive of magnificence, on account of the exalted rank held by the heads of the ancient monastic orders, was never again conferred, but was replaced by the lowlier title of *Master.*

If this partition of the world among a few men appear extraordinary, the attendant circumstances were still more so. The new apostles set out on foot, destitute of money and all human resources, intrusted with the double mission of preaching, and founding monasteries. One of their number, Juan de Navarre, refused these conditions, and demanded money. Dominic, seeing a Friar Preacher so distrustful of Providence, threw himself weeping at the feet of this son of little faith, but, unable to conquer his distrust, ordered twelve deniers to be given him.

Just as these arrangements were completed, the aged Raymond re-entered Toulouse on the 13th of September 1217, exactly four years after the battle, of Muret. The work of the Abbot of Cîteaux was destroyed, and that of God completed.

CHAPTER XI.

Dominic's fourth journey to Rome—Founding of the monasteries of St. Sixtus and St. Sabine, and accompanying miracles.

D OMINIC did not quit Languedoc immediately after the dispersion of the Friars. This is proved by an agreement concluded by him on the 11th of the following September, respecting the tithes previously assigned to him by Foulques. There was a query as to the extent of these rights, and it was decided that the tithes should not be exacted from any parish containing less than ten families, and arbiters were appointed to settle any future difficulties. This done, Dominic crossed the Alps on foot, with no companion but Etienne de Metz. History loses sight of him until he arrives at Milan, where he is seen at the door of the College of Saint-Nazaire asking hospitality of the Canons, by whom he was at once received in virtue of his Canon's dress.

On arriving in Rome, his first care was to find a suitable locality for his monastery. At the southern base of Mount Cœlius, facing the gigantic ruins of the Baths of Caracalla in the Appian Way, was an ancient church dedicated to St. Sixtus II., Pope and martyr, near whose remains five other Martyr-Popes were interred. On one side of the church, recently

restored, stood an unfinished cloister. The profound
solitude of the spot contrasted strangely with the
newly erected work, which had evidently been suddenly interrupted. This was indeed the case, as the
restoration of this ancient and celebrated edifice had
been suspended by the death of Innocent III., who
had destined this cloister for the abode of those nuns
who were then living in Rome under too lax a rule.
Dominic, ignorant of this intention, hastened to ask
the Sovereign Pontiff to grant him the church and
monastery. Honorius III. acceded to this request.

In three or four months Dominic had gathered together at Saint Sixtus as many as a hundred
Religious. The slowness of action, hitherto characteristic of his career, was now succeeded by a marked
rapidity; and though only commencing his career at
the age of twenty-five, and spending twelve years in
the formation of sixteen disciples, he now saw them
falling at his feet as ripe grain before the reaper's
scythe. There is nothing marvellous in this; for it is
a law of nature and grace that a force long sup-
pressed acts with impetuosity when its barriers are
removed; and in everything there is a point which,
once attained, renders success prompt and inevita-
ble. Situated on the road by which the Roman
conquerors proceeded to the Capitol, Saint Sixtus
witnessed, during a whole year, scenes far more marvellous than any the Appian Way had ever yet
beheld. Never did Dominic show clearer manifesta-
tions of the power God had given him over the souls
of men, and never did nature render him more reverent obedience. This was the triumphant moment of

his life.

First of all, there was the monastery to be completed; and whilst that work was going on, Dominic resumed his preaching in the churches and his instruction in the Vatican. Each day brought him some new disciple, with whom he peopled the habitable portion of his monastery; the morning saw him issue forth, staff in hand, and at evening he returned, bringing home his spoil; thus the progress of the spiritual and material building was simultaneous. Satan, jealous of such success, wished to mar its progress. One day when the Friars were engaged in showing to an architect an arch that needed restoration, or removal, the structure gave way, burying a workman beneath the ruins. The Friars, overwhelmed with grief, and distressed as to the state of the poor man's soul, and the unfavourable impression that might result from this untoward event, knew not what course to take. Meanwhile Dominic arrives, has the body removed from beneath the ruins, and on its being laid at his feet, invokes Him who has promised always to hear the prayer of faith, and in answer to his petition returning life animates the mangled form.

On another occasion the procurator of the monastery, Jacques de Melle, was so dangerously ill that the last sacraments had been administered to him. The Friars were gathered round his bed, praying for his departing soul, and sorrowing over the loss of a man so useful to them, inasmuch as he was better known in Rome than any of their number. Dominic perceiving his children's grief, commanded every one to quit the room, closed the door, and being left alone with the sick man, prays so fervently that the dying man revives, and Dominic, summoning the Friars, gives him back healed.

As the monastery possessed no revenues, it was the procurator's duty to provide, with the aid of Providence, for the needs of the community, who subsisted on the daily alms collected from street to street by the Friars. One morning Jacques de Melles told Dominic that there was nothing for dinner save two or three loaves of bread. Dominic appeared delighted at these tidings, and ordered the procurator to divide that little, according to the number of inmates, into forty portions, and to have the dinner-bell rung at the usual hour. On entering the refectory, each person found a mouthful of bread set before him, and grace having been said more joyously than ever, they sat down. Dominic was at the Prior's table, his heart upraised to God. After a moment's delay, two young men clothed in white appeared in the refectory, and advancing to Dominic's table, placed on it the loaves they carried in their mantles.

The same miracle occurred later on, attended by circumstances which we must allow the lips of antiquity to relate. "While the Friars were yet residing in the church of Saint Sixtus, in number about one hundred, the blessed Dominic one day ordered Friar Giovanni de Calabria and Friar Alberto Romano to go and seek alms in town. Three o'clock arrived and they had received nothing; they were returning home, and had already reached the church of Saint-

Anastasia, when a woman, much devoted to the Order, met them, and seeing that they had nothing, gave them a loaf, saying, 'You shall not return empty handed.' A little farther on they were accosted by a man who earnestly besought them for alms; they replied that they had nothing for themselves, and therefore had nothing to give him. The man still persisting, they said to one another, 'One loaf is of little use to us; let us give it to him for the love of God.' They then gave him the bread, and he disappeared instantly. Now, as they were about to re-enter the monastery, the holy Father, to whom the Holy Spirit had already revealed all that had taken place, met them, saying with a joyous air, 'Children, have you nothing?' 'No, father,' they replied, and then they related to him all that had happened, and how they had given their only loaf to the poor man. Dominic replied, 'It was an angel of the Lord; the Lord will provide for His own; let us pray.' Thereupon he entered the church, and coming out after a little while, told the two Friars to summon the community to the refectory. They replied, 'But, holy Father, how will you that we call them, when there is nothing to eat?' and they purposely delayed executing his order, so that the blessed Father sent for Brother Roger, the cellarer, and ordered him to summon the Friars to dinner, for the Lord would supply their needs. The tables were therefore laid, the cups were set, and at a given signal the whole community entered the refectory. The blessed Father said grace, and when every one was seated, Brother Enrico Romano began to read. The blessed Dominic continued praying, his clasped hands resting on the table, when behold, in answer to a promise made him by the Holy Spirit, two beauteous young men, ministers of Divine Providence, appeared in the midst of the refectory, carrying loaves in two white cloths suspended from their shoulders. They began with the lower ranks, placing before each brother a whole loaf of singular beauty. Then, coming to the blessed Dominic, they placed a loaf before him, bowed and disappeared, without any one ever knowing, even to the present day, whence they came or whither they went. The blessed Dominic addressed his children, saying, 'My brothers, eat the bread which the Lord has sent.' He then told the lay brothers to pour out the wine, but they replied, 'Holy Father, there is none.' Then the blessed Dominic, full of the prophetic spirit, said unto them, 'Go to the cask, and give the Friars the wine the Lord has sent.' They went, and found the cask filled to the brim with excellent wine, with which they speedily returned. And the blessed Dominic said, 'My brothers, drink the wine that is sent you by the Lord.' Then they ate and drank as much as they liked, that day and the morrow and the day following. But after the meal of the third day he ordered all the remaining bread and wine to be given to the poor, and none to be kept. During those three days no one had gone seeking alms because the Lord had sent an abundance of bread and wine. After this the blessed Father preached a beautiful sermon to the Friars, bidding them never distrust Divine Providence, even in the hour of the greatest penury. Friar Tancred, Prior, Friar Odo, and Enrico of Rome, Friar

Laurence of England, Friar Gaudione, and Friar Giovanni Romano, and many others were present at this miracle, which they related to Sister Cecilia and to other sisters then residing in the convent of Santa-Maria-Tras-Tevere, and to whom they even gave portions of the bread and wine, which were preserved for a long time as sacred relics. Friar Alberto, sent by the blessed Dominic to beg in company with another, was one of the two whose death Dominic had predicted. The other was Friar Gregorio, a man of singular beauty and grace; he was the first to die, and entered the presence of the Lord after receiving the last sacraments. On the third day after his death, Friar Alberto, having also received the sacraments, went from this gloomy prison to the celestial palace."[1]

This ingenuous narrative reveals the inner life of Dominic's family, and makes us realise the early character of the Order far better than any description could do. We behold how populous monasteries arose without the aid of gold and silver; how faith supplied the want of fortune; how exquisite was the simplicity of those men, many of whom had been the denizens of palaces. Friar Tancred, Prior of Saint-Sixtus, was a knight of lofty birth, attached to the Imperial court of Frederic II. Chancing to be in Bologna early in the year 1218, at the time that some of Dominic's Friars were there, as we shall see later on, he one day began suddenly to reflect on the danger of

---

[1] Sister Cecilia's Narrative, n. 3.

losing his soul. Troubled by this thought, he had recourse to the Blessed Virgin, who on the following night appeared to him in a dream, saying, "Enter my Order." Upon this he awoke, but falling asleep again, beheld two men habited as Friar Preachers, one of whom, an aged man, addressed him thus: "Thou hast besought the Blessed Virgin to show thee the way of salvation; come to us and thou shalt be saved."[1] Tancred, to whom the Order was as yet unknown, deemed that what he had seen was an illusion. Next morning he arose, and entreated his host to conduct him to a church, so that he might hear mass. He was taken to a small church called Santa-Maria-de-Mascarella, recently given to the Friar Preachers; and scarcely had he crossed the threshold when he met two Friars, one of whom he recognised as the old man of his dream. Having set his affairs in order, he took the habit and joined Dominic in Rome.

Friar Enrico, also alluded to by Sister Cecilia, was a young Roman noble, whose friends were so indignant at his joining the Order that they determined to carry him off. Dominic, knowing their resolve, dispatched the young man with a few companions, bidding them take the Nomentan Way. His friends followed and reached the banks of the Anio just as Enrico had crossed. The latter, seeing how great was his danger, raised his heart to God, entreating help for Dominic's sake. The waters at once rose with rapidity, the knights vainly essaying to cross the stream. When they had withdrawn, Enrico quietly

---

[1] Gerard de Frachet, *Vie des Frères*, Book iv. ch. xiv.

returned to Saint-Sixtus.

Friar Laurence of England, another witness of the miracles, had been sent to Paris on the dispersion of the Friars, but returned soon after with Juan of Navarre. Two others, Dominic de Segovia and Miguel de Uzéro, had also returned from Spain, after an apparently fruitless mission. It was Honorius's intention to carry out his predecessor's design, and reunite in one convent and under the same Rule the nuns scattered among the religious houses of Rome. This intention he imparted to Dominic, considering him the most capable of accomplishing so difficult an undertaking. Dominic readily acceded to the Holy Father's proposition, seeing in it a means, not only of restoring Saint-Sixtus to its primitive destination, but also of founding a community of Dominican nuns, after the model of Notre-Dame-de-Prouille. His only request was, that some of the Cardinals should be associated with him, in order to give weight to the undertaking. The Pope granted him three, Ugolino, Bishop of Ostia, Stefano di Fosso-nuovo, and Nicolai, Bishop of Tusculum, and in exchange for Saint-Sixtus gave him the church and monastery of Santa-Sabina on the Aventine Mount, close to his own abode. Simultaneous preparations were at once made for the reception of the Friars at Santa-Sabina and for the nuns at Saint-Sixtus.

Though busied with this twofold charge, Dominic still continued his preaching. One day a woman left her sick child in order to hear him preach at San Marco, and on returning home, found her child was

dead. Her hope was as great as her grief; and, accompanied by a servant carrying the child, she
hastened to Saint-Sixtus without giving herself time
to shed a single tear. On entering the court of Saint-
Sixtus by the Appian Way, the church and monastery
were at your left, and in front was the low and isolated building called the Chapter-house. At this door
Dominic was standing when the poor mother arrived.
She ran straight to him, seizing the child, laid it at
his feet beseeching him to restore it to life. Dominic
withdrew for a moment into the Chapter-house, then
returning to the threshold, made the sign of the cross
over the child, and, stooping down, took it by the
hand and restored it to the mother, charging her to
tell no one what had just occurred. Nevertheless the
news spread rapidly, and the Pope desired that the
miracle should be proclaimed from every pulpit.
Dominic opposed this, threatening to turn to the hea-
then and quit Rome for ever. But silence could not
be enforced, and Dominic was held in higher veneration than ever. Wherever he went he was followed
by the nobles and people, who regarded him as an
angel of God, and esteemed themselves happy if they
might touch him. They had cut so many pieces from
his cloak, in order to preserve them as relics, that it
scarcely reached his knees. And when the Friars endeavoured to prevent this destruction of his
garments, he replied, "Let them do it; it is a proof of
their love." [1]

The miracle was witnessed by the Friars Tancred,

---

[1] Sister Cecilia's Narrative, n. 1.

Odo, Enrico, Alberto, and many others.

Notwithstanding the striking proofs of Dominic's sanctity, the proposed re-union of the nuns at Saint-Sixtus met with much opposition. The majority of them refused to sacrifice the liberty they had hitherto enjoyed of quitting their cloister and visiting their friends. But God came to His servant's aid. At that time there was a convent in Rome, named, on account of its position, Santa-Maria-Tras-Tevere, in which was preserved one of those pictures of the Blessed Virgin attributed by tradition to St. Luke. This picture was held in great veneration by the people, inasmuch as when carried in procession by St. Gregory the Great, it had arrested the plague then ravaging the city, and the popular belief was, that on being placed in the Basilica of St. John Lateran, it returned of its own accord to its former abode. The Abbess of the above-named convent, and all the nuns, save one, voluntarily offered themselves to Dominic, to whom they made a vow of obedience, on the sole condition of their bringing the picture of Our Lady with them; if the picture returned voluntarily to its former abode, then their vow of obedience should be annulled. This condition was accepted by Dominic, who, in virtue of the authority with which they had just invested him, forbad them henceforth to quit their convent. These Religious belonged to some of the noblest families in Rome, and when their friends learnt the character of the new project and the nature of the vows taken, they hastened to Santa-Maria in order to dissuade the nuns from fulfilling their promise. They were so blinded by passion that they treated Dominic as an unknown adventurer, and so unsettled the nuns that many of them repented of their vow, Dominic, inwardly conscious of all that was going on, came to see them one morning, and after saying Mass and preaching, addressed them as follows: "My daughters, I know that you regret your decision, and that you desire to quit the heavenly road; let such as remain faithful, renew their vow." [1] Then all of them, headed by their Abbess, made a fresh profession of obedience. Dominic took possession of the keys of the convent, placed lay-brothers to guard the building day and night, and prohibited the nuns holding any conversation whatsoever without the presence of a third party.

Matters being at this point, Cardinals Ugolino, Stefano di Fosso-nuovo, and Nicolai assembled at Saint-Sixtus on Ash Wednesday. The Abbess of Santa-Maria, accompanied by the nuns, was there in order to make a solemn resignation of her office and cede all the rights of the convent to Dominic and his Friars. "Then when the blessed Dominic and the cardinals were seated, and the Abbess and her nuns were assembled, a man rushed in, tearing his hair, and uttering loud cries. They asked him what was the cause of his grief, and he replied, 'Monsignor Stefano's nephew has just been thrown from his horse, and killed.' The young man's name was Napoleon, and his uncle, on hearing his name, fell senseless on Dominic's breast. The bystanders supported him, and Dominic, arising and sprinkling him

---

[1] Sister Cecilia's Narrative, n. 13.

with holy water, ran to the spot where lay the young man, horribly shattered and mangled. He ordered him to be removed to a room and left there. Then he told Friar Tancred and the others to make preparations for Mass. The blessed Dominic, the Cardinals, Friars, the Abbess and the nuns proceeded to the spot where the altar was, and the blessed Father celebrated Mass, weeping all the time. At the moment of the elevation of the Sacred Host, the astonished spectators beheld Dominic raised a cubic from the ground. Mass ended, he returned to the body of the dead man, accompanied by the Cardinals, the Abbess, nuns, and bystanders, and approaching the corpse, composed its limbs with his own sainted hands, then prostrated himself on the ground, praying and weeping. Thrice he arranged the limbs of the deceased, and thrice he prostrated himself on the ground. Having arisen for the third time, he made the sign of the cross over the dead man, and standing at his head, with hands outstretched to heaven and his body elevated more than a cubic from the ground, he cried with a loud voice, 'Napoleon, I command thee in the name of the Lord, arise!' Then, in sight of the astonished spectators, the young man arose safe and sound, saying to Dominic, 'Father, give me to eat.' The Blessed Dominic gave him food and drink, and restored him to his uncle the Cardinal, full of joy, and bearing no trace of injury."[1]

Four days later, on the first Sunday in Lent, the nuns of Santa-Maria, of Santa-Bibisana, and of other

[1] Sister Cecilia's Narrative, n. 2.

convents, and some people of the world, entered
Saint-Sixtus, where they received the habit from
Dominic's hands. They numbered forty-four in all,
and among them was a sister of Santa-Maria, aged
seventeen, and called Cecilia. She it is to whom we
are indebted for the leading events of the holy Patriarch's life at this epoch, which events have been
preserved in an account written at her dictation, and
which is in itself a *chef-d'œuvre* of simplicity and
truth.

The picture of the Blessed Virgin was removed to
Saint-Sixtus on the evening of the day in which the
nuns entered that convent. Night-time was selected,
as the inhabitants of Rome disapproved of the removal.   Dominic, accompanied by the Cardinals
Stefano and Nicolai, and preceded and followed by
many persons with torches in their hands, bore the
picture on his shoulders. All were barefooted, and
the nuns were on their knees in Saint-Sixtus, awaiting the picture, which was happily installed in the
church.

All these events, including the journey to France
and Rome, are comprised within the space of five or
six months, and between 11th September 1217 and
the commencement of the following March. Yet, despite his numerous avocations, Dominic still found
time for private acts of charity. He often visited the
recluses, women who voluntarily seclude themselves
within holes of walls, and never quitted those abodes.
A few of them were scattered here and there throughout the town, on the desert sides of Mount Palatine,
in the gloomy interior of disused towers, and beneath

the broken arches of aqueducts; such were the ruined
posts where the sentinels of eternity kept watch.
Dominic visited them at sunset, bearing a ray of comfort expressly reserved for them. After discoursing
to the multitude he turned his steps to the abode of
solitude. One of these recluses, named Lucia, living
behind the church of Santa-Anastasia, on the road to
Saint-Sixtus, and whose arm was eaten to the bone
by a dreadful disease, was healed one evening by
Dominic's blessing. Another, whose breast was de-
voured by worms, lodged in a tower near the gate of
St. John Lateran. Dominic confessed her, and
brought her the Holy Eucharist from time to time.
On one occasion he requested to see one of the worms
which tormented her, and which she lovingly cherished in her bosom as heaven-sent guests. Bona,
such was her name, consented to Dominic's wish, but
the worm was transformed into a precious stone in
Dominic's hand, and Bona's breast became pure as
that of a babe.

Dominic was then at the zenith of his his maturity, his body and soul having reached that point
when age has but perfected their vigor. "He was of
middle height, and thin, his countenance beautiful,
and his complexion rather florid; hair and beard
blonde, and his eyes beautiful. From his brow and
from between the eyebrows issued a radiant bright-
ness commanding respect and love. He was always
joyous and happy, save when moved by compassion
at the sight of other's sorrow. His ands were long,
and beautifully formed, his voice loud, noble, and so-
norous. He never became bald, and his tonsure was

entirely surrounded by beautiful white hair."[1]

Thus is he depicted by St. Cecilia, who knew him in the heroic days of Saint-Sixtus and Santa-Sabina.

---

[1] Sister Cecilia's Narrative, n. 14.

CHAPTER XII.

St. Dominic at Santa-Sabina—St. Hyacinthus and the Blessed Celsus enter the Order—Our Lady anoints the Blessed Reginald.

THE CHURCH of Santa-Sabina, near which the Friars had resided since their departure from Saint-Sixtus, was built on the Aventine Mount. An ancient inscription records its foundation during the Pontificate of Celestine I., at the commencement of the fifth century, by a priest of Illyria named Peter. It is situated on the loftiest and steepest part of the hill. The murmuring Tiber, as it hurries away from Rome, leaves the narrow shore at its base, dashing its waves against the ruins of the bridge Horatius Cocles defended against Porsena.

Two rows of ancient columns, supporting a simple roof, divided the church into three aisles, each terminated by an altar. It was a primitive basilica, beautiful in its simplicity. The relics of Santa-Sabina, who suffered martyrdom in the reign of Adrian, reposed beneath the high altar, as near the scene of her martyrdom as tradition would allow. Close to her shrine were other precious relics. The church adjoined the palace of the Sabelli, then occupied by Honorius III., and from which the Bull authorizing the Order of Friar Preachers was dated.

From the windows of this building, part of which had been just ceded to Dominic, the very heart of Rome could be discerned, and the view was bounded by the hills of the Vatican. Two winding slopes led into the town, one descending to the Tiber, the other ending at one of the angles of the Palatine, near the church of Santa-Anastasia. This was the route which Dominic traversed in going from Santa-Sabina to Saint-Sixtus. No path on earth preserves so many traces of his steps. Almost daily, for more than six months, he ascended and descended the hill, passing from one convent to the other, impelled by the ardour of his charity.

On entering Santa-Sabina, one of the *chefs-d'œuvre* of Rome even at the present day, and carefully examining the naves, the traveller discerns ancient frescoes on the walls of a side chapel. One of these frescoes represents Dominic conferring the habit of his Order on a young man kneeling at his feet, whilst another figure is extended on the ground; the faces of both are hidden, and yet the spectator is profoundly moved. These two young men are Poles, Hyacinthus and Celsus Odrowaz. They had accompanied their uncle, Yve Odrowaz, Bishop-elect of Cracow, and having been conducted to Saint-Sixtus, probably by Cardinal Ugolino, Yve's fellow-student in the University of Paris, had witnessed the restoration to life of the young Napoleon. The Bishop at once entreated Dominic to let him take some Friar Preachers back with him to Poland. The Saint replied that having none who understood the language or customs of that country, the better way to propagate the Order there and in the North would be for some of the Bishop's suite to take the habit. Hyacinthus and Celsus offered themselves readily. It is supposed that they were brothers, and it is certain that they were related. They were of kindred heart as well as of kindred blood; both had been dedicated to Jesus Christ by the priestly office; both had glorified their Master in the eyes of their fellow-countrymen, and their virtues were but heightened by their youth. Hyacinthus was a canon in the church at Cracow, Celsus was provost of the church at Sandomir. Both of them took the habit at Santa-Sabina, with two other of their travelling companions, known in Dominican history under the name of Henry the Moravian and Herman the Teuton. On that mysterious hill, not comprised by the Romans within their sacred enclosure, and the name of which denotes *the home of birds*,[1] Poland and Germany, till then the sole countries that had proffered no sons to Dominic, now laid their tribute at his feet.

How grand and simple are the ways of God! Ugolino Conti of Italy and Yve Odrowaz of Poland met at the University of Paris, where they both passed some portion of their youth; then time, which strengthens or destroys friendship, as it does all other things, separated them for the space of forty years. Yve, promoted to the episcopacy, is obliged to go to Rome, and recognises in one of the Cardinals the friend of

---

[1] "Dirarum nidus domus opportune volucrum."—*Virg. Æn.* lib. viii.

his early days. The Cardinal conducts his guest to
the church of Santa-Sabina, in order to introduce
him to a man whose name Yve had never heard, and
that same day this man's virtue is unexpectedly revealed by the most supreme act of power, displaying
sovereignty over life and death. Yve, overcome by
the sight of this miracle, petitions Dominic to grant
him a few of his Friars, little dreaming that he had
journeyed to Paris and to Rome in order to lead to
Dominic four noble children of the North, predestined by God to found monasteries of Friar Preachers
in Germany, Poland, Prussia, and even in the very
heart of Russia.

Hyacinthus and his companions only remained a
short time at Santa-Sabina. As soon as they were
sufficiently instructed in the rules of the Order, they
set out with the Bishop of Cracow, and in passing
through Friesach, a town of ancient Norica, between
the Drave and the Murthe, they were moved by the
Holy Ghost to announce to the people the Word of
God. The country was stirred to its very depths by
their preaching, and, encouraged by their success,
they resolved to found a monastery in that place. It
was completed in six months, and they then left it
and its numerous inmates under the direction of Herman the Teuton. On their arrival at Cracow, the
Bishop gave them for their monastery a wooden
house belonging to the See. Such were the first fruits
of the Order in the regions of the North. Celsus
founded the monasteries of Prague and Breslau, and
before his death Hyacinthus extended the Order as

far as Kiev, in the very sight of the Greek schismatics, and amid the din of the Tartar invasions.

The South and North seemed to vie with each other as to who should send Dominic the most celebrated labourers. There was in France a doctor called Reginald, who had taught canonic law in Paris during five years, and who was Dean of the Chapter of Saint-Aignan-d'Orléans. In the year 1218, he went to Rome to visit the tomb of the Apostles, proposing afterwards to go to Jerusalem and render homage at the Holy Sepulchre. This twofold pilgrimage was intended by him as the prelude of a new life which he intended to embrace. "God had inspired him with the desire of quitting all things to preach the gospel, and he prepared himself for this work, though not knowing in what way to fulfil its duties; for as yet he had not heard that a preaching Order had been instituted. Now it happened that in a private interview with one of the Cardinals, he opened his heart to him on this matter, saying that he was thinking of quitting all to preach Jesus Christ in a life of voluntary poverty. Then the Cardinal replied, 'An Order has just arisen whose aim is to unite the practice of voluntary poverty with the office of preaching, and at this moment the Master of the new Order is in this town, preaching the Word of God.' Having heard this, Master Reginald hastened to find the blessed Dominic and reveal to him the secret of his soul. Entranced by the sight of the Saint and by the grace of his conversation, he resolved on entering the Order. But adversity, the test of all holy undertakings, delayed not to prove his. He fell so dangerously ill, that nature seemed about to succumb, and the physicians despaired of saving his life. The blessed Dominic, grieved at so soon losing this new child, urgently besought divine mercy; according to his own words, when relating the fact to his Friars, not to rob him of a child rather conceived than born, but to spare him if only for a little time. Whilst praying thus, the Blessed Virgin, Mother of God and Mistress of the world, with two young companions of matchless beauty, appeared to Master Reginald as he was lying awake, consumed by the violence of fever, and he heard the Queen of Heaven saying, 'Ask what thou wilt, and I will grant thy request.' Deliberating as to his reply, one of the Blessed Virgin's young companions counselled him to make no request, but leave all to the will of the Queen of mercy, to which suggestion he willingly agreed. Then the Blessed Virgin extended her pure hand, anointed his eyes, ears, nostrils, lips, hands, reins, and feet, accompanying each anointing with appropriate words. I have only been able to learn those used in anointing the reins and feet: 'May thy loins be girt with chastity, and thy feet with the gospel of peace.' Then she showed him the habit of the Friar Preachers, and saying, 'Behold the dress of the Order,' disappeared, leaving Reginald perfectly restored, the result of the anointing bestowed by her who has the secret of all healing. On the morrow, when Dominic came to ask him how he was, he replied that he was quite well, and he related the vision. Then both rendered devout thanksgiving to Him who wounds and who heals, who casts down and who raises up again. This sudden and unexpected recovery astonished the physicians, who knew not who had effected the cure."[1] Three days after, as Reginald was sitting with St. Dominic and a Religious of the Order of Hospitallers, the miraculous anointing was renewed in presence of the two latter, as if the august Mother of God attached such importance to this act that she desired to perform it openly. Reginald was but the representative of the Order of Friar Preachers, and in him the Queen of heaven and earth contracted alliance with the whole Order. As the Rosary had been the first sign of this union, and was the jewel conferred on the Order at its baptism, so the anointing bestowed on Reginald, sign of virility and confirmation, must also have a durable and commemorative sign. Therefore the Blessed Virgin in presenting to the new brother the habit of his Order, presented not the habit as it was then worn, but with remarkable alteration, which we must explain.

We have already stated that Dominic, who had for a long period been one of the Canons of Osma, continued to wear his Canon's habit, and adopted it as the dress of his Order. It consists of a white woollen tunic, covered by a linen surplice, both of which were enveloped by a cloak and hood of black wool. Now, in the vestment shown to Reginald by Our Lady, the linen surplice was replaced by a woollen scapular, i.e., a simple band of stuff, intended to cover the shoulders and chest, and descending as far as the

---

[1] The Blessed Humbert, *Vie de St. Dominic*, n. 27.

knees. This scapular was not new. It was already known to the monks of the East, by whom, doubtless, it had been adopted to replace the cloak when labour or heat obliged them to lay it aside. Desert-born and the offspring of modesty, the scapular falling as a veil over the heart of man has become in Christian tradition the symbol of purity, and therefore the dress of Mary, Queen of virgins. This is why (when anointing the whole Order in the person of Reginald) the Blessed Virgin girt them with the girdle of chastity, and shod their feet with the gospel of peace; she also presented them with the scapular, as the external sign of those angelic virtues without which it is impossible either to discern or to announce heavenly things.

After this remarkable event, one of the most noteworthy in Dominican history, Reginald set out for the Holy Land, and the linen surplice was exchanged for the woollen scapular, henceforth the distinctive mark of the Order. On a Friar Preacher making his profession, his scapular only is blessed by the Prior who receives his vows, and in no case may he leave his cell without wearing his scapular—not even when carried to his last home. At this same epoch the Blessed Virgin gave another proof of her maternal love for the Order. "One evening, Dominic was praying in the church until midnight, at which hour he entered the corridor where the Friars were asleep in their cells. Having finished his business, he resumed his prayers at the end of the corridor, when chancing to turn his eyes to the other end, he beheld three women approaching, the centre one being the most beautiful and venerable. One of her companions carried a magnificent vase, and the other an aspersorium, which she presented to her mistress, who sprinkled and blessed all the Friars save one. Dominic, after noting who the Friar was, advanced to meet the woman, who had already reached the middle of the corridor, near the lamp suspended in that spot. He prostrated himself at her feet, and although he had recognised her, entreated her to tell him her name. At that time, the beautiful and devotional anthem of the *Salve Regina* was not yet sung in the monastery and nunnery of the Order in Rome, but only recited, kneeling, after Complin. The woman replied, 'I am she whom you invoke every eve, and when you say, *Eia ergo, advocata nostra*, I prostrate myself before my Son, entreating Him to protect this Order.' The blessed Dominic then asked who her two companions were, on which the Blessed Virgin said, 'One is Cecilia, and the other Catherine.' The blessed Dominic then inquired the reason of her omitting to bless one of the Friars, and she replied, 'Because he was not in a becoming posture.' Then having finished her round, and sprinkled and blessed the Friars, she disappeared. The blessed Dominic returned to the spot where he had been praying, and hardly had he recommenced his devotions when he was raised in spirit to the presence of God. He beheld the Lord, having at His right hand the Blessed Virgin, who seemed to Dominic to be robed in a sapphire-coloured mantle. Looking round and discerning Religious of every Order but his own, he began to weep bitterly, not daring to approach our

Lord or his Blessed Mother. Our Lady motioned him
to draw near, but he dared not comply until encouraged by our Lord. Then he approached and
prostrated himself weeping bitterly. The Lord said,
'Why weepest thou so bitterly?' and he replied, 'Because I see here members of every Order but my
own.' The Lord said to him, 'Dost thou wish to see
thy Order?' He tremblingly replied, 'Yes, Lord;' and
the Lord rested His hand on the shoulder of the
Blessed Virgin, saying to Dominic, 'I have confided
thy Order to my mother.' Then He added, 'Wilt thou
indeed see thy Order?' to which Dominic replied,
'Yes, Lord.' Then the Blessed Virgin unfolding her
mantle in Dominic's sight, so that it covered the
whole of the celestial abode, he beheld beneath it a
multitude of his children. The blessed Father prostrated himself to render thanks to God and to our
Lady, and the vision disappeared. As he recovered
consciousness, the bell was ringing for Matins, and
when they were ended, he convoked a chapter of his
Friars, and discoursed to them on the love and veneration they ought to have to the Blessed Virgin, and
among other things he related this vision. At the
close of the chapter, he privately took aside the
brother whom Our Lady had not blessed, and gently
asked him if he had not kept back something in the
general confession he had made. He replied, 'Holy
Father, my conscience accuses me of nothing, save
that last night, when I awoke, I found I had been
sleeping with no garments on.' At Saint-Sixtus the
blessed Dominic related his vision to Sister Cecilia
and the others, as if it had been beheld by another

person, but the Friars present made a sign to the sisters that it was Dominic who had seen it. It was on this occasion that the blessed Dominic enjoined that, wherever they slept, the Friars should wear their girdle and their sandals."[1]

In Lent, on the second Sunday after the sisters' removal to Saint-Sixtus, Dominic preached in their church before a vast concourse of people, and exorcised a woman who was disturbing the congregation by her shrieks. On another occasion, having arrived unexpectedly at the convent gate, he questioned the portress as to the health of Sisters Theodora, Theadrana, and Nimpha, and on hearing that they were ill of fever, he enjoined the portress to "tell them from me that I command them to recover."[2] The portress obeyed, and as soon as she gave the Saint's message, they found themselves cured.

It was the venerable Father's constant habit to devote the whole day to winning souls, either by fervent preaching, by the confessional, or other works of charity. In the evening he came to the sisters, and in presence of the Friars gave them a discourse or conference on the duties of the Order, he being their sole instructor on this point. One evening when he was late in coming, and the sisters having ceased to expect him, finished their prayers and retired to their cells, suddenly the brothers rang the little bell announcing the Father's arrival. The sisters hastened

---

[1] Sister Cecilia's Narrative, n. 7.
[2] Sister Cecilia's Narrative, n. 9.

to the church, and on opening the grille, beheld Dominic already seated with the Friars, and awaiting them. The blessed Dominic addressed them thus: "My daughters, I have been fishing, and the Lord has sent me a fine fish." By this he meant Gaudione, whom he had received into the Order, and who was the only son of a certain nobleman named Alessandro, a citizen of Rome and a grand man. Then having made them a long and consolatory discourse, he said, "My daughters, I think it would be well to take something to drink." And summoning Brother Roger, the cellarer, ordered him to fetch some wine and a cup. When Roger had done this, the blessed Dominic told him to fill the cup to the brim; then, having blessed it, he drank of it first, and then all the other Brothers present, in number about twenty-five, and consisting of clerics and lay brothers; they drank as much as they liked and yet the cup remained full. When all had partaken of the wine the blessed Dominic said, "I wish my daughters also to take some." And calling Sister Nubia; told her to "go to the door, take the cup, and give the sisters to drink." She went with a companion and carried the cup, which, although brim-full, did not run over. The Prioress drank first, then all the sisters took as much as they wished, the blessed Father often saying, "Do not hurry, my daughters." There were more than four hundred of them, and though they all drank as much as they chose, the wine did not diminish, and when brought back the cup was as full as at first. That done, Dominic said, "It is the Lord's will that I go to

Santa-Sabina." But Friar Tancred, Prior of the Friars, Friar Odo, Prior of the Nuns, the Friars, the Prioress, and all the nuns endeavoured to detain him, saying, "Holy Father, it is nearly midnight and too late for you to go." Nevertheless he refused to accede to their request, replying, "The Lord wills me to go, and He will send His angels with us."

CHAPTER XIII.

Founding of the Monasteries of Saint-Jacques-de-Paris and San-Niccolà-di-Bologna.

THE FRIARS sent to Paris by Dominic, after the meeting at Prouille, separated into two bands. The first, consisting of Mannis, Miguel de Fabra, and Odéric, reached their destination on the 12th September; the second, consisting of Matthieu de France and Laurence of England, arrived three weeks later. They took up their abode in the centre of the city, near the Hospital of Notre-Dame and the Archbishop's palace. They were all strangers to Paris save Matthieu de France, part of whose youth had been passed in the schools of the university. For the space of ten months they lived in extreme poverty, but consoled by the thought of Dominic, and by a revelation vouchsafed to Laurence of England respecting their future.

At that time Jean de Barastre, Dean of St. Quentin, royal chaplain, and professor at the University of Paris, had founded at one of the city gates, called the Narbonne or Orleans gate, a hospice for poor foreigners. The chapel of the hospice was dedicated to the Apostle St. James, so celebrated in Spain, and whose shrine is one of the most renowned in Christendom. Whatever the cause that attracted the Spanish Friars to this spot, whether devotion or otherwise, Jean de Barastre learnt that there were in Paris some new Religious, preaching the gospel in the apostolic manner. He made their acquaintance, admired and loved them, and doubtless was impressed with the importance of their institute, seeing that on the 12th August 1218 he put them in possession of the Hospice of St. James, which, in the person of poor strangers, had been dedicated by him to our Lord, who rewarded him by sending guests far more illustrious than he had counted on. The lowly hospice at the Orleans gate became a home of apostles, a school of savants, and a royal tomb. On the 3rd of May 1221, Jean de Barastre officially confirmed the donation made to the Friars, and at the request of Honorius III. the University of Paris ceded their rights in that place, stipulating that their doctors should after their decease participate in the suffrages of the Order, in the same manner as did the members of the Order, and this in right of confraternity. Being thus provided with a permanent and public abode, the Friars began to be better known. The people came to hear them preach, and they made many conquests among the numerous students who from all parts of Europe brought to Paris the ardour of their youth and the varying genius of their respective countries. In the summer of 1219, the monastery of St. Jacques contained thirty inmates. Of those who took the habit at that time, one name alone has been handed down, that of Henri de Marbourg. Many years previously he had been sent to Paris by his uncle, a pious knight residing at Marbourg. After his decease, this uncle appeared to Henry in a dream, saying, "Take the Cross, in expiation for my sins, and pass the sea. On your return from Jerusalem you will find a new Order of preachers in Paris, and you will join their band. Let not their poverty or the fewness of their numbers alarm you, for they will become a numerous people, and will be for the salvation of many souls."[1] Henry crossed the sea, and returning to Paris at the time when the Friars began to settle there, he unhesitatingly joined their ranks. He was one of the most celebrated preachers of the monastery of St. Jacques; St. Louis conceived a warm affection for him, and he accompanied the King to Palestine in the year 1254, and died on returning home with the monarch.

He relates the following trait relative to the early life of the Friars in Paris:—"One day the itinerant Friars having had no food until three in the afternoon, were consulting with one another how to appease their hunger. In the poor strange district they were traversing, a man in travelling attire addressed them, saying, 'O men of little faith! of what are you discoursing? Seek first the kingdom of God, and the rest shall be added unto you. You had faith sufficient to give yourselves to God; and do you fear that He will fail to nourish you? Cross this field, and when you reach the valley beyond, you will come to a village; you will enter the church, the priest of which will offer you hospitality, and then a knight will arrive, who will be so desirous of receiving you into his

[1] Gerard de Frachet, *Vie des Frères*, book iv. ch. 13.

house that he will almost carry you off by force, and the patrons of the church interceding, will take the priest and you into his house, where you will be magnificently entertained. Trust, then, in the Lord; and charge your Friars to do so too.' Having said this, he disappeared; and everything took place exactly as he had predicted. On returning to Paris, they related this incident to Friar Enrico and the few poor Friars then resident in that place."

Probably their extreme poverty was the cause why two of their number, Juan de Navarre and Laurence of England, joined Dominic in Rome in January 1218, when the Saint commanded Juan to proceed at once to Bologna in company of a Friar whom, to distinguish him from Bertrand de Garrigue, historians allude to as a "certain Bertrand." Shortly after they were joined by Michel de Uzéro and Dominique de Segovia, who had returned from Spain, and three other Friars, Richaud, Chretien, and Pierre, the last named being a lay brother. It is not known how this little colony obtained their house and church of Santa-Maria-de-Mascarella, where they resided in a state of extreme penury, unable to cope with this large city, where religion, business, and pleasure had each its allotted place, and which did not readily interest itself in anything new. The arrival of one man changed the whole aspect of affairs. Reginald appeared in Bologna on the 21st December 1218, on his return from Palestine, and soon the whole city was moved to its very depths.

Nothing equals the success of divine eloquence. In

eight days Reginald was master of Bologna; ecclesiastics,   jurisconsults,   university   students,   and
professors vied with each other in entering an Order
which only a few hours before was either despised or
unknown. Many clever men dreaded to hear the orator, lest they too should succumb to the power of his
word. An historian says: "When Friar Reginald, of
sainted memory, formerly Dean of Orléans, was
preaching at Bologna, drawing into his Order many
ecclesiastics and doctors of renown, Moneta, who was
Professor of Arts, and renowned throughout Lombardy, seeing so many conversions, began to fear for
himself, sedulously avoiding Friar Reginald, and in-
ducing his own pupils to do the same. But on St.
Stephen's Day they dragged him to the sermon, and
finding himself unable to resist, he said to them, 'Let
us go first to St. Procul and hear Mass.' They went,
and heard, not one Mass, but three. Moneta delaying
purposely in order to miss the sermon, but being hur-
ried by his pupils, consented to go. On arriving at
the church, the sermon was not yet over, and the
crowd being very great, Moneta was compelled to remain at the entrance. Scarcely did the preacher's
voice fall on his ears than he was conquered. The
orator was exclaiming at that moment, 'I see heaven
open! yes, heaven is open to all who desire to see and
to enter; its gates are open to all who wish to pass
within. Close not your heart, nor lips, nor hands, lest
heaven be closed too. Why still delay? Heaven is
open now.' As soon as Reginald left the pulpit, Moneta, moved by the Spirit of God, went to him,
acquainted him with his position and calling, and

took the vow of obedience. But having many engagements to complete, he retained his secular garb for more than a year, with Reginald's consent, and labouring all the time to augment the number of the latter's auditors and disciples, seemed himself to take the habit with each new conquest that he made."[1]

As the monastery of Santa-Maria-de-Mascarella was too small for the Friars, Reginald, by the interposition of Cardinal Ugolino, then Legate Apostolic in those parts, obtained from the Bishop of Bologna the church of San-Niccolà, situated near the walls, and surrounded by fields. The chaplain of the church, a God-fearing man, named Rodolfo, far from disapproving the Bishop's generosity to the Friars, himself took the habit. He said that before the arrival of the Friars in Bologna, there was a poor woman, despised of men, but loved of God, who often knelt in prayer near a certain vineyard where the monastery of San-Niccolà was afterwards established, and when derided for praying with her face turned towards that spot, replied, "Oh! miserable fools that ye are! Did you but know what kind of men will dwell there one day, and what events will transpire on that spot, you would fall on your knees and thank God; for the whole world will be illumined by those who will dwell there."[2]

It is related by another Friar, Giovanni di Bologna, that lights and brilliant apparitions were often

---

[1] Gerard de Frachet, *Vie des Frères*, Bk. iv. ch. x.

[2] Ibid., Bk. i. ch. iii.

seen by the labourers in the vineyard of San-Niccolà, and Friar Clarin remembers in his childhood passing one day near this vineyard with his father, who said to him, "My child, angelic songs have often been heard in this spot, and that always presages something wonderful." On the child remarking that perhaps they were human voices that had been heard there, his father replied, "My son, the voice of angels is different to the voice of men, and cannot be mistaken."[1]

Having removed to San-Niccolà in the spring of the year 1219, the Friars continued to multiply; thanks to the preaching of Reginald, the renown of their virtues, and the wonderful and repeated interpositions of Providence. A student at the university was called in the following manner. When asleep one night, he seemed to be alone in a vast field, when a violent storm arose. He ran to the nearest house, knocked, and asked for shelter; but a voice replied, "I am Justice, and because thou art not just, thou shalt not enter my abode." He then knocked at another door, where another voice answered, "I am the Truth, and cannot receive thee, because Truth shelters none but those who love her." He applied elsewhere, but was repulsed with the words, "I am Peace, and there is no peace for the wicked, but only for the man of good-will." Then he knocked at one door more, and a person opened it, saying, "I am Mercy; if thou desirest to escape the tempest, go to the monastery of San-Niccolà, where the Friar Preachers dwell; there

---

[1] Gerard de Frachet, *Vie des Frères*, Bk. i. ch. iii.

thou wilt find the stable of penitence, the crib of chastity, the food of doctrine, the ass of simplicity, the ox of discretion; Mary, who will enlighten thee; Joseph, who will aid thee; and Jesus, who will save thee." On this the student awoke, and regarding his dream as a warning from Heaven, complied with its admonitions.

It was not to any earthly attraction that the conversion of these young men and men of advanced age was due. Nothing could be more severe than the Friar's life. The poverty of a rising Order was experienced in many ways; mind and body, wearied by apostolic labour, were only repaired by fast and abstinence; the long day was succeeded by a short night and a hard couch. The slightest transgression of the Rule was severely punished. A lay brother having accepted, without permission, a piece of some coarse stuff, Reginald ordered him to bare his shoulders to receive the discipline in presence of the Friars. The culprit refused. Reginald made the Friars remove his garment, and raising his tearful eyes to heaven, said, "O Lord Jesus Christ, Thou who didst give to Thy servant Benedict the power of chasing the Evil Spirit from the body of his monks by the rod of discipline, grant me grace to vanquish this poor brother's temptation by the same means." Then he flogged him so severely that the Friars and all present began to weep.[1]

We can readily understand that nature was indeed vanquished in men capable of submitting to

---

[1] Gerard de Frachet, *Vie des Frères*, Bk. iv. ch. ii.

such treatment as this. And this victory obtained over self, by the stern repression of pride and the senses, helped them also to overcome the world. For what power could it henceforth possess over hearts thus fortified against shame and suffering? Admirable spectacle! Religion elevates man by the very means the world employs for his abasement. She by servitude renders him free, and by crucifixion she makes him a king. The penances of the cloister were not the severest trials experienced by the youthful and illustrious novices who thronged the gates of San-Niccolà. The strongest temptation in all new undertakings is found in their newness itself, and in the dimness of the horizon where float all nascent things. When any institution has weathered the storm of centuries, there issues from its stones an odour of stability, rendering the heart of man triumphant over doubt: he sleeps as peacefully as a child rocked on its grandsire's aged knees, and as securely as the moss on a vessel that has traversed the ocean a hundred times. But all new undertakings are in sad harmony with the human heart; they mutually disturb each other. San-Niccolà-di-Bologna was not screened from those violent tempests by which, in accordance to the law of Providence, all divine work in which man co-operates must be tried and purified. An historian relates: "At the time when the Order of Preachers resembled a small flock and a new plantation, the Friars in the monastery of Bologna were so tempted to lose heart that many of them conferred as to the Order they would enter, feeling sure that their own, so new and so feeble, could not exist long. Indeed, two of the leading Friars had obtained from an Apostolic Legate permission to join the Cistercians, and had presented the letters to Friar Reginald, formerly Dean of St. Aignan of Orleans, but at that time the blessed Dominic's Vicar. Friar Reginald having convoked the chapter, revealed the matter, appearing much afflicted; the Friars wept aloud, and deep grief took possession of all. Friar Reginald, mute, and with eyes upraised to heaven, spoke to none save God, placing all his trust in Him. Friar Clair di Toscano arose to exhort the Friars. He was a good man, a man of much influence, originally a professor of arts and canon law, and latterly Prior of the Roman Province, and penitentiary and chaplain to the Holy Father. Scarcely had he ended his discourse when Rinaldo di Cremona entered. He was a clever and celebrated doctor, teaching philosophy at Bologna, and was the first of the Friars to become professor of theology in Paris. He entered alone, and, filled with the Holy Spirit, at once demanded the habit. Friar Reginald, beside himself with joy, took off his own scapular, with which he invested Rinaldo. The sacristan rang the bell; the Friars hymned the *Veni Creator Spiritus*; and while singing it, their voices interrupted by tears of joy, the people hastened to the spot; numbers of men, women, and students crowded into the church. The whole town was moved by the report of what had occurred; renewed regard was evinced for the Friars; every temptation vanished; and the two Friars who had resolved on quitting the Order, rushing into the chapter, resigned the apostolic permission they had received, and promised to persevere even unto death."[1]

Such was the early history of Niccolà-di-Bologna and Saint-Jacques-de-Paris, both of them corner-stones of the Dominican edifice. The two most celebrated universities of Europe fostered beneath their wings that chosen band of preachers and of doctors, and, in accordance with the original text of its constitutions, deputies from every province of the Order annually assembled in one or other of the abovenamed localities, where, from age to age, there existed men surpassed by none of their contemporaries—men who continued to win for the Order the respect due from those for whose welfare it laboured, San-Niccolà-di-Bologna had the honour of witnessing the closing years of Dominic's life, and of being his last resting-place. Saint-Jacques-de-Paris likewise became the site of a celebrated tomb. Tenderly loved by St. Louis, it received beneath its marble the remains of a number of French princes, Robert, the sixth son of St. Louis, and founder of the Bourbon line, was baptized there by the Blessed Humbert, fifth Master-General of the Order, and also buried there. His son and his great-grandson were likewise interred in that spot, and their united remains formed but one tomb, on which was graved this epitaph: "Here is the root of the House of Bourbon; the first prince of their line lies here; this tomb is a cradle

---

[1] Gerard de Frachet, *Vie des Frères*, Bk. i. ch. v.

of kings." [1]

Strange destiny! The monastery of St. Jacques, where, in the person of its founder, the House of Bourbon had been baptized, and where its four earliest generations reposed, was the spot whence issued the first blows which overthrew the throne of France; the most implacable destroyers of monarchy assembled within its deserted cloister, and the name which the French Dominicans had borne, thenceforth became a name of sanguinary import. [2]

Now St. Jacques is not even a ruin; a number of houses and sheds cover its ignoble relics; and in such indifference is the spot held, that probably the House of Bourbon no longer knows that its earliest ancestors lie buried there.

---

[1] *"Hic stirps Borbonidum. hic primus de nominee princeps conditur. hic tumuli velut incunabula regum."* This inscription was written by Santeuil.

[2] It was not really in the monastery of St. Jacques, but in another Dominican monastery, near the centre of the Rue St. Honoré, that the Jacobin Club held its meetings.

CHAPTER XIV.

*Dominic's journey to Spain and France—His vigils in
the grotto of Segovia—His manner of travelling
and mode of life.*

A FTER a laborious year spent in founding San-
Sisto and Santa-Sabina, Dominic turned his
gaze towards those distant countries throughout
which his first children were scattered. He longed to
see them again, to fortify them by his presence, and
with them to bless God for the good and evil His
hands had bestowed.

In the autumn of 1218 he set out, accompanied by
a few members of his own Order, and was afterwards
joined by a Minorite Friar named Albert. Having arrived at some place in Lombardy, they stopped at an
inn and seated themselves at table with the other
guests. On the meat being handed round, Dominic
and his companions refused to take any, and the
hostess seeing that they contented themselves with
bread and a little wine, grew violently angry, ad-
dressing insulting language to the Saint. In vain
Dominic tried to appease her by his patience and his
edifying conversation; and as none of the party could
stem the torrent of her maledictions, he at last said
to her gently, "My daughter, in order that you may
learn to receive the servants of God in a charitable

manner for their Master's sake, I pray the Lord Jesus
to impose silence on you." He had hardly finished
speaking when the hostess became dumb. On re-
passing the same spot, on his return from Spain,
eight months later on, he was recognised by this
woman, who cast herself at his feet, entreating pardon by her tears. Dominic made the sign of the cross
on her lips, and immediately her tongue was loosed.
Friar Albert, who related this event, also says that
on Dominic's tunic being torn by a dog, the Saint
joined the torn part with a little mud, and so repaired
the damage.

Having crossed the Alps, Dominic found himself
once more in Languedoc, traversing its well-known
roads. But all was changed. He had not even the
consolation of praying at the tomb of his magnani-
mous friend the Count of Montfort, whose remains
had been transported to the Abbey of Fontevraud, far
from that territory where he had been crowned Duke
and Count, and where his now lifeless sword could
no longer protect his coffin. After a passing greeting
to Saint-Romain-de-Toulouse and to Notre-Dame-de-
Prouille, Dominic hastened to his native land, whose
soil had been untrodden by him for a space of fifteen
years. He left it a simple Canon of Osma; he returned an apostle, thaumaturgist, founder of an
Order, legislator, patriarch, destroyer of the heretics
of the day, and one of the most valiant servants of
truth and of the Church. But this glory was his only
possession. Any one meeting him in the gorges of the
Pyrenees, his face turned towards Spain, would have
taken him for a foreign beggar going to bask in the

glorious Iberian sun. Whither did he first wend his
steps? Was it to the Vale of Duero? Was he looked
for in the palace whence death had chased his par-
ents? Was he going to pray at their tomb at Gumiel
d'Izan, and at that of Azévédo at Osma? Did the Abbey of San-Domingo-de-Silos behold him on his knees
on that pavement where his mother had been consoled by enigmatic presages? History gives no reply,
and we need no words of hers to tell us what the
Saint's heart has already revealed. From Jesus
Christ he had learnt to elevate, without destroying,
the natural sentiments of the human heart. The first
place where we find him in Spain is a proof of the love
he had retained for his native land. History presents
him to us at Segovia, one of the chief towns of Old
Castile, and situated not far from Osma. He lodged
in the house of a poor woman, who soon discerned the
treasure she possessed. Since his abode in Languedoc he had been accustomed to wear a rough
garment, of wool or hair. Whilst in Segovia he laid
aside his inner garment of wool, in order to substitute one of harder texture. His hostess, aware of the
fact, took possession of the left-off garb, which she
reverently deposited in a chest; and on her room taking fire one day during her absence, everything was
consumed, save her most valued possessions, the
chest and the garment it contained.

Another miracle awoke the gratitude of the inhabitants of Segovia. Although it was the Christmas of
the year 1218, a prolonged drought had prevented
the land being sown. The people gathered together
outside the town to offer their united supplications to

God that He would send them rain. Dominic stood up in the midst of the crowd, and after a few words which seemed ineffectual in soothing their alarm, exclaimed, "Cease your fears, my brethren, and trust in the mercy of God, who will this very day send you an abundant rain, and will change your mourning into joy."[1] Although no sign of rain had been visible, the heavens grew dark, the clouds gathered, and the Saint's words were interrupted by a violent rain which dispersed the crowd. The people of Segovia erected a chapel in honour of this miracle, on the spot where it occurred.

On another occasion, Dominic attended a council of the principal inhabitants of the town, and after the royal letters had been read, addressed the assembly as follows: "Brethren, you have just listened to the words of a terrestrial and mortal king, now hear the commands of the Heavenly and Eternal One." On this a nobleman angrily exclaimed, "Does this prater mean to keep us here all day and hinder our dinner?" He then turned his steed homewards, the servant of God saying, "You withdraw now, but ere the year is ended your horse shall be riderless, and in vain will you seek to escape from your enemies by fleeing to the tower you have built."[2] This prophecy was accurately fulfilled; ere the year closed, he, and his son, and one of his relatives were killed on the very spot where he was when Dominic addressed him as above.

Segovia lies between two hills separated by a

---

[1] Gerard de Frachet, *Vie des Frères*, Bk. ii. ch. vi.

[2] Ibid., Bi. ii. ch. vii.

river. On the one to the north, where the city walls
did not extend, Dominic discovered a desert cave, fit
spot for the mysteries of penance and contemplation.
On this hill he founded the monastery of Santa-Cruz,
and whilst its humble walls were being erected the
Saint used the adjoining cave as his nocturnal ora-
tory, for he was in the habit of consecrating part of
the night to prayer and other spiritual exercises. The
day he gave to his fellow-creatures, to preaching, and
to business; but when the sun began to set, he too
quitted the world, finding in the Divine Presence the
bodily and spiritual refreshment he needed. After
compline he remained in the choir, taking care that
none of the Friars should follow his example, unwilling to set them one too difficult for them to follow, or
from a holy modesty that made him shrink from their
discovering the secret of his intercourse with God.
But curiosity won the day; taking advantage of the
darkness, several Friars hid themselves in the
church in order to witness his vigils, the touching details of which were thus learnt. On finding himself
alone, protected by the silent darkness, he would un-
fold his heart to God. The church, type of the
heavenly and eternal city, seemed to him to be en-
dued with life and capable of being moved by his
entreaties, groans, and tears. He passed round, stopping to pray at each altar, either making a profound
obeisance, or prostrated or kneeling on the ground.
It was generally in the former manner that he began
his adoration of our Lord, as if the altar, sign and
memorial of His sacrifice, were indeed His very person. Then prostrating himself with his face to the

ground, he was heard uttering these words of the Gospel, "*God be merciful to me a sinner;*" and those of David, "*My soul cleaveth to the ground; give me life according to Thy word;*" and many similar passages. Rising, he gazed intently at the Crucifix, genuflecting a certain number of times, alternately gazing and adoring. From time to time this silent contemplation was interrupted by the following ejaculations: "*Lord, to Thee have I cried, turn not Thy face from my petition, but listen to my cry,*" and other expressions drawn from Holy Writ. Sometimes his genuflections were prolonged; no words passed his lips; he seemed to see heaven open, and the tears streamed down his cheeks, his breast heaving with emotion, as does the traveller's on nearing his native land. At other times he stood erect, his hands stretched out before him as a book, in which he seemed to read attentively, when he would raise them on each side as far as the shoulder in the attitude of a man listening, or veil his eyes in order to meditate more profoundly. At times he was seen standing on tiptoe, his face heavenwards, and his hands clasped above his head in the form of an arrow; then he would separate them as if asking something, and then close them as if he had received what he desired; and in this state, seeming no longer a denizen of earth, he was wont to say, "Lord, hear my voice whilst I cry unto Thee, whilst I lift up my hands to Thy holy temple." There was one mode of praying adopted by him, but rarely, and only when he desired to obtain some extraordinary favour from God; it consisted in standing erect with his arms and hands outstretched in the form of a cross, as those of our dying Lord were extended when He sent up to heaven those loud cries that saved the world. He would then say in a grave and clear voice, *"Lord, to Thee have I cried, to Thee have I stretched out my hands all day long; my soul is in Thy sight as a thirsty land; hear me, and that right speedily."* Thus did he pray when he restored the young Napoleon to life; but those present did not hear the words he used, nor did they dare to ask him what they were.

Besides the private supplications with which each day's needs and events inspired Dominic, the cause of the Universal Church was ever present to his mind. He prayed for the extension of the faith in the heart of Christians, for those in the bondage of error, and for the souls in purgatory. "So intense was his love for souls," says one of the witnesses in the process of his canonisation, "that it not only extended to all the faithful, but to unbelievers, and even to those suffering in hell, for whom he shed many tears." [1] Tears did not suffice; thrice each night he mingled his blood with his prayers, thus satisfying, as far as he could, that thirst for immolation which is the generous part of love. They heard him flogging himself with knots of iron, and the grotto of Segovia, which witnessed all the severity of his penances, has retained for centuries the traces of his blood. It was divided by him into three parts: one for his own sins, the second for the sins of the living, and the third for the sins of the departed. More than once he con-strained some of the Friars to strike him in order to

---

[1] *Actes de Bologne*, deposition of Fr. Ventura, n. 9.

augment the humiliation and pain of his sacrifice. A day will come when, in presence of heaven and earth, God's angels will place on the altar of judgment two full cups; an unerring hand will weigh them both, and, to the eternal glory of the saints, it will be known that each drop of blood given by love will have spared torrents of the same.

When Dominic had spent a long space of time in vigils, prayers, and tears, and had offered his soul and body as a sacrifice, if the matin bell had not rung, he would go and visit his children, as if longing to see them again. He would enter their cells very quietly, making the sign of the cross on each of the inmates, and re-covering those whose clothing had become disarranged in sleep. After this he returned to the choir. Sometimes he would be overtaken by sleep during the pious mysteries of his night, and he would be found leaning against an altar or extended on the ground. When the matin bell rung, he joined the Friars, and going from one to the other side of the choir, exhorted them to sing joyously and heartily. The Office ended, he withdrew to sleep in some corner of the house, for, unlike the other Friars, he had no cell of his own, but would throw himself down, all dressed as he was, on the nearest object, whether bench, straw, bare ground, or, as sometimes happened, even on a bier. So brief was his nightly rest, that he often fell asleep at table during his meal. On quitting Segovia, where he left Friar Corbalan as Prior, Dominic came to Madrid. There he found a monastery already begun, by the instrumentality, it is supposed, of Pedro de Madrid, one of those sent to Spain by

Dominic on the dispersion of the Friars. It was situated outside the walls of the town. Dominic changed its destination by making it a convent, and dedicated it to San-Domingo-de-Silos. But in time the name of Silos was lost, and by one of those imperceptible transformations for which the world is responsible, the convent afterwards bore the founder's name. It is worthy of note that as in France and Italy, so in Spain also the holy Patriarch was as zealous in founding convents as monasteries, ever mindful that Notre-Dame-de-Prouille was the first-fruit of his labours. A lasting proof of his solicitude for the inmates of the Madrid convent is to be found in a letter addressed to them soon after their establishment there, and which runs as follows:—"Friar Dominic, Master of the preachers, to the Mother Prioress, and to the nuns of the convent in Madrid, health and amelioration of life by the grace of our Lord Jesus Christ. We rejoice greatly and render thanks to God for your spiritual advancement, and because He has drawn you from the mire of this world. By prayer and fasting strive, my daughters, against your old enemy, for only he who strives lawfully shall be crowned. Until lately you possessed no suitable dwelling in which to carry out the rules of the Order, but now you are without excuse, seeing that by God's grace you now have an abode in every way appropriate to the exact fulfilment of the Rule. Therefore I desire that silence be henceforth observed in all places designated by the constitutions of the Order, viz., in the choir, refectory, and corridors, and that elsewhere you live according to your Rule. Let none of you pass through the convent gate, nor any enter there, unless it be a bishop or prelate coming thither to preach or to make a public visit. Neglect not vigils and discipline, be obedient to your Prioress, and lose no time in vain conversation. As it is impossible for us to provide for your temporal wants, we desire that they may not be augmented, and we therefore forbid any Friar whatsoever to receive any novices at your expense; but the Prioress shall have power to do this at the desire of the convent. We ordain that our dear brother Mannès, to whom you and your convent are so much indebted, shall arrange, regulate, and order all things in the manner he may deem most conducive to your advancement in the religious life. We empower him to visit and correct you; and if he judge it necessary, and the majority of the nuns consent, even to depose your Prioress. He may also grant you dispensations according to his own discretion. Farewell in Christ."

Many other monastic houses in Spain claim the honour of having been founded, directly or indirectly, by Dominic. As early historians are silent on this point, we deem it unnecessary to allude to claims hardly warranted by the brevity of Dominic's sojourn in Spain. We shall only mention Palencia, where the Saint passed ten years of his early life, and where it appears certain that he established a Confraternity of the Rosary and a monastery named San-Paulo.

At Guadalaxara, not far from Madrid, while on his way to France, Dominic was deserted by all the brothers who had accompanied him, save Friar Adam and two lay brothers. Turning to one of them, he asked if he also intended to desert him. "God forbid," replied the brother, "that I should leave the head and follow the feet!"[1] This defection had been announced to Dominic in a vision. He prayed for the lost sheep, and had the consolation of seeing nearly all of them return to the fold. It was probably in their behalf that, when nearing Toulouse, and when they had but one cup of wine for eight persons, he miraculously augmented it, "moved by compassion," say the historians, "at sight of some of the Friars who had been delicately brought up."[2]

At Toulouse Dominic met Bertrand de Garrigue, one of his earliest disciples. They travelled together en route for Paris,[3] visiting on their way the celebrated Roc-Amadour, an ancient sanctuary dedicated to Our Lady, and built on a steep and rocky solitude of Quercy. "After passing the night in prayer, they were joined on the morrow by several German pilgrims, who having heard them singing psalms and litanies, reverently followed them on their way. At the nearest village their new companions invited them to dinner, and continued their hospitality for four days running. On the fifth day the blessed Dominic addressed Bertrand de Garrigue, and, sighing, said, "Brother Bertrand, I am uneasy in conscience, seeing that we reap temporal things of these pilgrims, without bestowing on them any spiritual gifts. Therefore, if you please, we will

---

[1] Vincent de Beauvais, *Miroir Histor.*, Bk. xxx. ch. lxxvii.

[2] Gerard de Frachet, *Vie des Frères*, Bk. ii. ch. v.

[3] In vol. i. of the *Annales des Frères Prêcheurs*, by Mamachi, p. 60, Appendix.

kneel down and ask God for grace to understand and
speak their language, so that we may preach the
Lord Jesus to them." That done, to the pilgrims'
great surprise, they began to speak in German, and
during the four remaining days that they travelled
together, and until they reached Orleans, they discoursed to them of the Lord Jesus. At Orleans, the
pilgrims took the road to Chartres, after bidding
farewell to Dominic and Bertrand and commending
themselves to their prayers, and the latter proceeded
to Paris. Next day the blessed Father said to Bertrand, "Brother, we are now at Paris; if the Friars
learn the miracle the Lord has wrought, they will
look on us as saints, while in reality we are but sinners, and if the world hear of the miracle, our
humility will be in danger; therefore I forbid you to
mention it to any one until after my death."[1]

One of the first houses that greeted Dominic's
gaze on entering Paris by the Orleans gate was that
of St. Jacques. It then contained thirty Religious.
The holy Patriarch only stayed there a few days, during which time he bestowed the habit on the young
Guglielmo di Montferrat, whose acquaintance he
made at the residence of Cardinal Ugolino, and to
whom he promised that he should enter the Order,
after studying theology for two years at the University of Paris. Dominic kept his word. He also made
a new friend in the person of a native of Saxony
named Jourdain. He was a frank, eloquent, amiable,
and God-fearing youth. He was born in the diocese

---

[1] Gerard Frachet, *Vie des Frères*, Bk. ii. ch. x.

of Paderborn, was a member of the noble House of
Ebernstein, and had come to Paris to drink of the
fountain of divine knowledge. Moved for some time
by the Spirit of God, who destined him to succeed
Dominic in the general government of the Order, he
felt himself drawn to that great man, whose heir he
was to be, and who discerned how ardent was the impression made by Jesus Christ on the young man's
heart. In spite of his ordinary decision of action,
Dominic, fearing lest he should hurry the work of
grace in this predestined soul, counselled the young
Saxon to try the yoke of the Lord, by entering the di-
aconate, and left him to be matured beneath the
winds of Heaven, until the moment when the
reaper's hand should gather him in.

The courage and decision with which Dominic ha-
bitually acted was never manifested more clearly
than by the results attendant on his brief sojourn at
St. Jacques. The continuous exertion of several worthy men had during the year gathered together
thirty Religious, and the aim of this rising community was to increase its members by its own
individual efforts. Dominic arrives, casts one glance
at the little band of Frenchmen, and deems it sufficient to people France with Friar Preachers. At his
voice, Pierre Cellani sets out for Limoges, Philippe
for Rheims, Guerric for Metz, Guillaume for Poitiers,
a few others for Orleans, commissioned to preach and
found monasteries in those towns. Pierre Cellani
was diffident, and pleaded his ignorance and want of
books. Dominic replied, trusting confidently in divine help, "Go, my son, and fear not; twice a day will

I remember thee before God. Do not doubt. Thou wilt win many souls; thy harvest shall be abundant; thou shalt increase and multiply, and the Lord will be with thee." Pierre Cellani afterwards related, in the intimacy of friendship, that whenever he experienced any trouble, remembering this promise, he invoked God and Dominic, and all his efforts were crowned with success.

Dominic quitted Paris by the Burgundy gate. At Chatillon-sur-Seine he restored to life the nephew of an ecclesiastic, in whose house he was then lodging. The child had fallen from an upper story, and was found half dead. The uncle gave a grand banquet in the Saint's honour. Dominic, observing that the child's mother ate nothing because she was suffering from an attack of fever, offered her some eel that he had blessed, telling her to eat it in God's strength. She did so, and was cured at once.

"After that the glorious Father returned to Italy, accompanied by a lay brother named Jean. While traversing the Italian Alps, this brother grew so faint from hunger that he could neither walk nor even rise, from the ground. The pious Father said, 'My child, what is the matter? why can you not walk?' He replied, 'Holy Father, I am dying of want' The Saint rejoined, 'Take courage, my son; let us walk a little farther, and we shall find something: to refresh us.' But on the brother replying that he was unable to advance a single step, the Saint, with his usual kindness and commiseration, had recourse to his usual refuge—prayer. He uttered a short petition, and

turning to the brother, said, 'Arise, my son; go to yon-
der spot, and bring back what you will find there.'
The brother arose with extreme difficulty, and
dragged himself to the spot indicated, distant about
a stone's-throw. There he beheld a loaf of wonderful
whiteness, enveloped in very white linen. He took it
back, and, in obedience to the Saint's commands, ate
of it until he found himself refreshed. When he had
finished, the man of God asked him if he could continue his journey, now that his hunger was appeased,
and he replied that he could do so. 'Arise, then,' said
he; 'wrap up the remaining portion of the loaf in the
cloth, and take it back to the spot where you found
it.' The brother obeyed, and they went on their way.
When they had gone a little distance, the brother,
suddenly recollecting himself, exclaimed, 'O my God!
whence did that bread come, and who placed it in
that spot? I must have been beside myself not to
have wondered at this before.' And he said to the
Saint, 'Holy Father, whence came that loaf, and who
put it there?' Then this genuine lover and observer
of humility replied, 'My son, have you eaten as much
as you desired?' He answered, 'Yes.' 'Then,' rejoined
the Saint, 'if you have done so, thank God, and do not
trouble about the rest.'"[1]

We will stop at this spot, where Dominic's companion lost courage, and examine more closely the
traces of those steps whose path we also tread.

Dominic travelled on foot, a staff in his hand, and

---

[1] Gerard de Frachet, *Vie des Frères*, Bk. ii. ch. vi.

a bundle of clothes upon his shoulder. When in uninhabited spots, he walked barefooted, and when hurt by a stone would say laughingly, "This is our penance."[1] Once, when travelling with Friar Bonvisi, they arrived at a place bristling with sharp stones, when the Saint exclaimed, "Ah! once I was unfortunately obliged to put on my shoes here." And on the brother asking why he had done so, he replied, "Because there had been a great deal of rain."[2] On approaching a town or village, he would put on his shoes, keeping them on until he had passed through; and when a river or a torrent had to be traversed, he, making the sign of the Cross over the waters, would fearlessly enter the stream, setting an example to his companions. If it began to rain, he would sing aloud the *Ave Maris Stella* or the *Veni Creator Spiritus*. He carried no money with him, leaving himself to the mercy of his fellow-creatures and of Providence. He preferred lodging in monasteries, when that was practicable. He never consulted his own inclination as to when to rest, but yielding in this respect to the fatigue or wishes of his companions. He ate whatever was set before him, meat always excepted; for even when travelling, he rigorously observed the days of abstinence and fasting, although he dispensed his companions from the same. The more he was maltreated, the happier he felt. When sick, he ate roots and fruit, rather than partake of more delicate dishes. When obliged to dine with people of the

---

[1] *Actes de Bologne*, deposition of Jean de Navarre, n. 3.
[2] Third deposition of Bonvisi di Piacenza.

world, he first quenched his thirst at some fountain, fearing lest he might drink more than was becoming in a Religious, and so doing, might give scandal to those present. Sometimes he begged his bread from door to door, always humbly thanking the donors, occasionally even on his knees. He slept on straw or on a plank, and without undressing.

When travelling, he omitted none of his religious duties. If a church was at hand, he daily offered the Holy Sacrifice, and that amid floods of tears, so impossible was it for him to celebrate the Divine Mysteries without deep emotion. When the moment drew near that heralded the advent of Him, whom, from his early years, he had transcendentally loved, his whole frame thrilled, and tears streamed rapidly down his pale and radiant face. He uttered the *Pater Noster* in a manner so seraphic, that it manifested the near presence of the *Father who is in Heaven*. He enjoined silence on his companions in the morning until nine o'clock, and again after Compline. During the intervening time he spoke of God, his discourse assuming the form of conversation or of theological controversy, and every other imaginable form. Sometimes, especially in solitary places, he requested his companions to remain at a little distance, gently repeating those words of the prophet Osee, *"I will lead them into the wilderness, and there will I speak to their heart."* He either preceded or followed, meditating on certain passages of Scripture. On these occasions the Friars observed that he often passed his hand before his face, as if to drive some

troublesome insects away. His marvellous acquaintance with Holy Writ is attributed to this practice of
frequent meditation. So imbued was he with the consciousness of the Divine Presence, that he hardly
ever raised his eyes from the ground. He never entered any house as guest without first praying in a
church, if one was to be found in that locality. After
finishing his repast, he withdrew to a room in order
to read St. Matthew's Gospel or St. Paul's Epistles,
which he always carried with him. After sitting
down, he opened his book, made the sign of the Cross,
and began to read attentively. So enraptured was he
by the Divine Word, that he appeared beside himself;
gesticulated as if holding converse with some one;
then appeared to be listening, arguing, and contend-
ing; alternately laughed and wept; then, after gazing
intently, would cast down his eyes, soliloquise, and
strike his breast. From reading he passed to prayer,
from meditation to contemplation; at times lovingly
kissing the book, as if grateful to it for the happiness
it conferred; then, becoming more and more enraptured with its sacred joys, he covered his face with
his hands and hood. When night arrived, he betook
himself to the church to practise his wonted vigils
and penance, and if there was no church at his disposal, he retired to some distant chamber, whence, in
spite of his precautions, his groans disturbed the
slumbers of his companions. He awoke them at the
hour of Matins, that they might recite their Office in
common; and when he was tarrying in any monastery, even of another Order, he would knock at the

cell-doors, exhorting the inmates to arise and descend to the choir.

He preached to all whom he met in the roads, towns, villages, châteaux, and monasteries. His words were the words of love. His protracted studies at Palencia and Osma had initiated him into all the mysteries of Christian theology, which, welling forth from the depths of his loving heart, carried conviction to the most obdurate. A young man, enraptured by his eloquence, asked him what books he studied. He replied, "My son, chiefly in the book of charity, for that teaches everything." [1] When in the pulpit, he often wept, and was generally full of that supernatural melancholy resulting from a deep insight into spiritual things. When he perceived the crowded roofs of distant towns and cities, the thought of human misery and sin so saddened his reflections that his face betrayed his grief. Love, joy, trouble, and serenity passed in rapid succession across his brow, rendering his countenance most attractive in its expressiveness. "He was amiable to all," said one of the witnesses in the process of his canonisation, "to rich and to poor, and to the numerous Jews and infidels of Spain, in which country he was beloved by all, save by heretics and the enemies of the Church, whom he convinced by his controversies and his sermons." [2]

---

[1] Gerard de Frachet, *Vie des Frères*, Bk ii. ch. xxv.

[2] *Actes de Bologne*, deposition of Jean de Navarre, n. 3.

CHAPTER XV.

Dominic's fifth journey to Rome—The Blessed Reginald's death—The Blessed Jourdain de Saxe enters the Order.

IT WAS IN the height of summer in the year 1219 that Dominic descended, for the last time, the steep declivities of the Alps, and beheld again that rich, vast plain in which he was destined to spend the greatest part of his life. His infancy and youth had been passed in Old Castile; the most perfect years of his maturity were given to Languedoc; Rome was the spot whither he was incessantly led by the ardour of his faith; Lombardy was destined to be his tomb. We know not by what route he travelled there; early historians are silent as to his itineracy, until his arrival in Bologna, where the Prior and Friars of San-Niccolà received him with great joy. His first act was one of disinterestedness. Odéric Gallicani, a citizen of Bologna, had recently made over to the Friars some very valuable lands. Dominic tore up the contract in presence of the Bishop, declaring that he desired that his children should beg their daily bread, and that he would never permit them to amass any riches. No virtue was so dear to him as poverty. The whole year round he only wore a tunic of coarse material, in which garb he was not ashamed to appear in the presence of the grandest nobles. He desired that his Friars should dress as he did; that their houses should be small; that neither silk nor purple should be worn, even at the altar; and that they should possess no vessels of gold or silver excepting the chalices. The same spirit pervaded the meals. Two dishes were served, but the Friars partook of only one. Rodolfo di Faenza, procurator of the Bologna monastery, relates that having sometimes augmented the daily fare during Dominic's stay, the Saint called him, and whispering in his ear, said, "Why do you kill the Friars with such an allowance as this?"

When, as sometimes happened, bread or wine failed, Friar Rodolfo sought out Dominic, who would tell him to go and pray, and would often accompany him to the church to pray likewise, and Providence did not forsake them, but sent a dinner for his children.

One fast day, when the whole community was seated in the refectory, Friar Bonvisi went to Dominic and told him that there was nothing to eat. The Saint raised his eyes and hands to heaven with a joyous air, thanking God that he was so poor. But soon two strange young men enter the refectory, one of them carrying loaves, and the other dried figs, which they distributed to the community. Another day, when there were but two loaves in the monastery, Dominic ordered them to be broken into small fragments; then he blessed the basket, and told the server to go round the refectory, and give each Religious two or three of these small pieces. When this was done, Dominic commanded him to go round a second time, and not to leave off until all had received enough. The Friars generally drank nothing but water, but they always endeavoured to have a little wine for those who were sick. One day the infirmary attendant complained to Dominic that there was no wine, and gave him the empty vessel. The servant of God began praying, as was his wont on such occasions, humbly exhorting the rest to do the same, and when the attendant took up the vessel, he found it full. Historians make but passing allusion to the joy of the Friars at Dominic's arrival in Bologna, but we can easily conceive the effect of his presence among those who, though as yet they knew him not, were nevertheless his sons. Then they beheld with their own eyes the Spaniard who had converted them to God by the lips of a Frenchman, and who, renewing the early wonders of the Church, had formed a band of apostles consisting of Christians of every nation. They beheld him, and his virtues, miracles, speech, and physiognomy far exceeded any pre-conceived idea that they had formed concerning him. And so great was the ascendancy he gained within and outside the monastery, that its numerous and pious inmates were greatly multiplied during his brief sojourn there. Nothing could be more singular than the manner in which Stefano the Spaniard was called to enter the Order. He himself relates it in the following words:—"Whilst studying at Bologna, Master Dominic arrived, and preached not only to the students, but to others also. I went to

him for confession, and was impressed by the kindness of his manner. One evening, as I was preparing
to sup in my hotel with my companions, he sent two
Friars, who told me that Friar Dominic requested my
presence, and desired I would come immediately. I
said I would do so directly after supper. They, replying that he expected me at once, I arose and followed
them to San-Niccolà, where I found Master Dominic
surrounded by many of the Friars, to whom he spoke,
saying, 'Teach him how to make the prostration.'
And when they had so done, I prostrated myself with
docility, and he gave me the habit of a Friar
Preacher, saying, 'I desire to arm you with weapons
with which you will fight against Satan all the days
of your life.' I was filled with surprise then, and
never do I recall the incident without wondering by
what instinct Friar Dominic had called me, and
clothed me with the habit of his Order; for never had
I spoken to him of entering religion, therefore must
he have been guided by some divine inspiration or
manifestation." [1]

As in Paris, so in Bologna, Dominic sent forth
many of his Friars to preach and to found monasteries in Northern Italy, always acting on his own
favourite maxim, *that seed must be sown and not
kept.* Milan and Florence received colonies of Friar
Preachers, and he judged it expedient that Reginald
should leave Bologna for Paris, hoping that his eloquence and renown would effect the final

---

[1] *Actes de Bologne*, deposition of Stefano the Spaniard, n. 2.

establishment of the Order in France. The Friars beheld Reginald's departure from Bologna with deep regret, weeping to be so soon severed from their *mother's breast*, for thus Jourdain de Saxe expresses himself, adding, "But all these things happened in accordance with the will of God. There was something indescribably marvellous in the way in which the blessed servant of God dispersed the Friars hither and thither throughout the Church, and this in spite of the remonstrances he received, by none of which was his courage ever dimmed by one shadow of hesitation. It seemed as if he were conscious of a success revealed to him by divine inspiration; and who can doubt that this was indeed the case? At first he had but few Friars with him, and those chiefly simple and illiterate men, whom he dispersed in small numbers throughout the whole Church, so that in the judgment of the children of the world, who try all things by the test of prudence, he, instead of building up a mighty edifice, was but destroying what was already begun. Dominic's prayers accompanied his children, who by the grace of the Lord greatly increased."[1]

Dominic also quitted Bologna about the end of October. Crossing the Alps in the direction of Florence, he tarried a while on the banks of the Arno, where Santa-Maria-Novella and San Marco, two celebrated monasteries of his Order, were to be founded. The Friars were in possession of a church, at the side of which dwelt a woman named Béné, notorious for her

---

[1] *Vie de St. Dominique*, ch. ii.n. 45.

abandoned life, whom God had chastised by abandoning her to the power of the Evil One. This woman was converted by Dominic's preaching, and by his prayers she was freed from the power of Satan. This very deliverance was the cause of her relapse, and on Dominic's return to Florence five years later, she confessed the evil consequences of her deliverance. Dominic gently asked whether she was willing to return to her former condition, and on her replying that she submitted herself to God's will and to his, the Saint besought God to do what was best for the salvation of her soul. In a few days' time the evil spirit began tormenting her anew, and the punishment of her previous transgressions became a source of merit and perfection. She eventually took the veil, and with it the name of Benedetta. It is also recorded that on Dominic's return she bitterly complained of an ecclesiastic, by whom she had been greatly persecuted on account of her attachment to the Order, and whose dislike to the Friars was grounded on the fact that the church, of which he had formerly been chaplain, had been given to them. Dominic replied, "Be patient, my daughter, for your persecutor will one day belong to us, and will labour much on behalf of the Order."[1] Events proved the truth of this prediction.

At Viterbo, Dominic met the Sovereign Pontiff Honorius III., who, on 15th November 1219, gave the Friars letters recommendatory to the Bishops and

---

[1] Constantin d'Orviéto, *Vie de St. Dominique*, n. 37.

Prelates of Spain, and on the 8th of December following to the whole hierarchy. Honorius also made a
formal donation of the monastery of San Sisto in
Rome to Dominic and his Friars, who, until that period, held it in virtue of a verbal concession only. As
the nuns were included in the Order, and were under
the temporal and spiritual administration of the
Master-General, this is doubtless the reason why no
mention is made of them in the deed of transfer. This
was not the Saint's first visit to Viterbo. Three years
before, as he was returning to France after the confirmation of his Order, he arrived there with
Cardinal Capocci, who gave him the chapel and monastery of Santa-Cruz, erected on a neighbouring hill,
as also an adjoining church which he was then building. The Cardinal had been warned in a dream to
erect this church in honour of Our Lady; his friendship for Dominic induced him to offer it to the latter,
even before its completion, fearing delay, lest anything should occur to divert him from his purpose.
Though he did not live to complete it, he secured it to
the Order, and under the name of Nostra-Signora-di-
Gradi it has become one of the most renowned monasteries of the Roman Province. Remains of the
ancient chapel of Santa-Cruz, where Dominic had often passed his nights, and where until the last
century traces of his blood were to be seen, are still
visible.

Dominic was in Rome at the commencement of the
year 1220. An historian mentions his having presented the nuns of San-Sisto with some ebony spoons
he had brought them from Spain. What simplicity in

so great a man! In the midst of the business and fatigue of a long journey of six or seven hundred
leagues, he thought of the poor nuns, and, in order to
gratify them, carried them back a souvenir of his native land. I say carried, for he would never permit
any one to relieve him of his baggage.

Reginald had arrived in Paris, where he preached
with all the power of eloquence and faith. He was,
next to Dominic, the highest luminary of the new Order. The eyes of all the Friars were fixed on him, and
though little anticipating how soon death would rob
them of their founder, they rejoiced to know that
there was another capable of carrying on his work.

God soon dispelled their loving hopes. Reginald
was attacked by a fatal malady, and that at the very
moment when most was expected from him. Matthew of France, Prior of St. Jacques, announced to
him the arrival of the last struggle, and asked
whether they should not administer extreme unction. He replied, "I do not fear the combat; I await it
joyously; and I look for the Mother of Mercy, who
with her own hands anointed me at Rome; but lest I
should appear indifferent to the ecclesiastical unction, I wish to receive it also."[1]

At that time the majority of the Friars were ignorant of the mysterious manner in which Reginald
had been called to enter the Order, for he had besought Dominic not to mention it during his life. But
the recollection of this signal grace recurring to his
mind at the moment of death, he felt compelled to

---

[1] Gerard de Frachet, *Vie des Frères*, Bk. v. chap. ii.

allude to it, and gratitude wrung from him a secret which his humility had concealed till then. Another of his previous sayings has been preserved to us by Matthew of France, who, having known his celebrity and the refinements of his former mode of life, expressed surprise at his having embraced so severe a rule: "There is no merit due to me," said he, "for I have always liked it but too well."[1]

The exact day of his death is unknown, but it was either late in January or early in February of the year 1220. At that time the Friars having no right of sepulture within their own church, Reginald's remains were interred in the neighbouring edifice of Notre-Dame-des-Champs. Miracles were wrought at his tomb, and during four centuries his relics were the object of a devotion that promised to be lasting. But in the year 1614, the church of Notre-Dame-des-Champs was given to the Carmelites of the Reform of St. Theresa, and the nuns removed Reginald's remains into the interior of their own cloister. In spite of the hereditary veneration in which he has been held by them, he became in time almost forgotten by the outside world; his memory and tomb became the secret of those who love and live in the past. Now his very tomb exists no longer; it disappeared together with the church and monastery of Notre-Dame-des-Champs; and the founder of the monastery of Bologna, him whom the Friars named *their Staff*, he whom the Blessed Virgin had called, and whose limbs she had miraculously anointed, and who gave

---

[1] Le. B. Jourdain de Saxe, *Vie de St. Dominique*, ch. iii. p. 46.

the last and hallowed form to our habit, for him, the Blessed Reginald, there exists no *cultus*, not even in that Order of which his whole life, his eloquence, and the number of his illustrious children render him one of the most striking ornaments.[1] Many illustrious scions sprang from that root, even on the very eve of Raymond's short and fatal illness.

We remember the Saxon student whom Dominic knew in Paris, and whose vocation, marked as it was, he feared to hasten. This precious flower, which, by a delicate presentiment, Dominic had reserved for the honour and consolation of the last days of one of the worthiest of his sons, was culled by Reginald's hand. The following is the description given by Jourdain de Saxe of his own, and his friend Henri of Cologne's entrance into the Order:—"The very night in which the sainted Reginald's soul entered the presence of the Lord, I, who, though not yet vested with the habit, had nevertheless taken the vows of the Order, beheld, in a dream, a ship having the Friars on board; suddenly the ship sank, but the Friars were saved. I think the vessel denoted Friar Reginald, whom the Friars regarded as their great stay. Another person saw in a dream a limpid stream, which suddenly ceased flowing and was replaced by two gushing fountains. Supposing that the vision had a hidden meaning, I felt too conscious of my own weakness to attempt its interpretation. All I know is

---

[1] These word only apply to the *cultus ratified by the Church*, for the Blessed Reginald has never ceased to be the object of a warm devotion, which it is hoped will one day be confirmed by the Holy See.

this, that while in Paris, Reginald received no other
profession than mine and that of Friar Henri, afterwards Prior in Cologne, a man whom I loved in the
Lord, and for whom I felt a deeper affection than I
ever experienced for any other person. He was indeed a vessel of honour, and of such perfection that I
never remember seeing any one more full of grace.
The Lord speedily recalled him to Himself, and therefore it will be well to make some mention of his
virtues.

"Henri was of distinguished birth, and when quite
young had been appointed a Canon of Utrecht. From
his earliest years he had been trained in the fear of
the Lord by a very holy man, also a Canon of the
same church, and by whose example Henri had been
taught to overcome the world by crucifying the flesh
and by the practice of good works. He made him
wash the feet of the poor, love the house of God, shun
evil, despise luxury, and love chastity. This young
man, naturally of an excellent disposition, willingly
bore the easy yoke of virtue; he grew in goodness as
in stature, seeming an angel in whom purity was in-
nate. He came to Paris, and soon the study of
theology drew his quick genius and well-balanced
mind from the pursuit of all other sciences. Often
meeting in the same hôtel, our acquaintance ripened
into deep friendship. Friar Reginald, of sainted
memory, was in Paris at the same time, and so impressed was I by his preaching, that I made a silent
vow of joining his Order, which seemed to me a sure
way of salvation, and such a one as I had pictured in

my own imagination, before I knew the Friars. Having made this resolution, I was desirous that the friend and companion of my soul should take the same vow, for in him I discerned all the qualities of nature and grace requisite for a great preacher. Though I met with opposition, I still continued to urge him, and at last persuaded him to go to Friar Reginald for confession. On his return I opened the prophecies of Isaias, and alighted on the following passage: *'The Lord hath given me a learned tongue, that I should know how to uphold by word him that is weary: He wakeneth me in the morning that I may hear His voice. The Lord hath opened my ear, and I do not resist: I have not gone back.'* [1] Whilst interpreting to him this passage, so descriptive of the state of his own heart, and which I pointed out to him to be a heavenly counsel, exhorting him to submit to the yoke of obedience, we noticed a little lower down these two words, 'Let us stand together,' which we regarded as an intimation not to separate from each other, but consecrate our lives to the same object. It was in alluding to this, that, in writing to me one day when he was in Germany and I in Italy, he said, 'Where now is the *let us stand together*? You are at Bologna and I at Cologne!' I replied, 'What greater merit and more glorious crown can we win than by sharing the poverty of Christ and His Apostles, and giving up all for love of Him?' Though his reason was convinced, his will still resisted.

---

[1] Isaias l. 4,5.

"The night on which we held the fore-named conversation, he went to hear Matins in Our Lady's Church, and remained there till daybreak, praying the Mother of our Lord to quench his rebellious spirit; but not perceiving any amelioration in himself, began to say, 'O Blessed Virgin! now I feel that thou hast no pity on me, and that there is no room for me in the assembly of Christ's poor ones.' This he said sorrowfully, feeling a desire to embrace poverty, the value of which, at the last day, had been manifested to him by our Lord in the following manner. He saw in a dream our Lord seated on His judgment throne, and two countless multitudes, of which one was already judged, and the other was passing judgment, with our Lord. Whilst with quiet conscience he calmly regarded this scene, one of those near the Judge suddenly pointed to him, exclaiming, 'What hast thou ever renounced for the Lord's sake?' This question filled him with consternation, as he had no answer to give. He desired to embrace poverty, but the requisite courage was wanting. He withdrew from the Church of Notre-Dame, sad at not having obtained the grace he had entreated. But at that same moment He who has regard unto the humble melted his heart; torrents of tears streamed from his eyes; he poured out his soul before the Lord; all obstacles vanished, and the yoke of Christ, which had formerly appeared so burdensome, now appeared, as in reality it is, light and easy. In his first transport of joy he arose and hastened to Friar Reginald, who at once received his vows. Then he came to me, and whilst gazing at the traces of tears on his angelic countenance, I asked him where he had been. He replied, 'I have vowed to the Lord, and I will fulfill my vow.' We deferred taking the habit until Lent arrived, and during the interim we gained another companion. Friar Leon, who afterwards succeeded Friar Henri as Prior.

"When the day arrived on which, by the imposition of ashes, the Church reminds the faithful that of dust they are made and to dust they shall return, we prepared to fulfil our vow. Our acquaintances knowing nothing of our intention, one of them, on seeing Friar Henri quit the hôtel, asked him whither he was going. He replied, 'I go to Bethany,' alluding to the meaning of the word in Hebrew, signifying '*house of obedience*,' We all three proceeded to St. Jacques, entering at the moment when the Friars were chanting '*Immutemur Habitu.*' Our visit, though unexpected, was nevertheless opportune, and we put off the old man to put on the new, the Friars chanting that which we were doing."[1]

Reginald did not see Jourdain de Saxe and Henri of Cologne take the habit. He had returned to God before this; like the aloe, which dies in flowering, and never sees its own fruit.

---

[1] *Vie de St. Dominique*, ch. iii. n. 47, &c.

CHAPTER XVI.

First General Chapter of the Order—St. Dominic's stay in Lombardy—Institution of the Third Order.

ALTHOUGH scarcely three years had elapsed since the dispersion of the Friars at Prouille, they already possessed monasteries in France, Italy, Spain, Germany, and even in Poland. By God's blessing they had flourished and multiplied. Dominic, having witnessed and aided their progress, thought it was now time to rejoice them by the sight of their own strength, and this not to excite them to vain satisfaction, but to encourage them in still more arduous labours, to ensure their unity, and give the finishing touch to the legislation by which they werf governed. He therefore convoked a General Chapter of his Order at Bologna, to be held at Pentecost in the year 1220. Dominic left Rome at the end of February or the beginning of March. He spent a few days at Viterbo with the Holy Father, from whom he received fresh proofs of affection, consisting of three letters addressed to the people of Madrid, Segovia, and Bologna, thanking them for their kindness to the Friars, and exhorting them to persevere in the same. These letters are respectively dated the 20th, 23rd, and 24th of March. On the preceding February he had written to the Religious of Notre-Dame-des-

Champs in Paris, congratulating them on having granted the Friars right of sepulture in their church. On the 6th of the following May he recommended them warmly to the Archbishop of Tarragona, and on the 12th he gave permission to the monks of different Orders to associate themselves with Dominic in the office of preaching.

On the day of Pentecost, Dominic was at Bologna, surrounded by the Friars of San-Niccolà, and by the representatives of the whole Order. We know the names of none, save that of Jourdain de Saxe, who on taking the habit had been sent from Paris with three other Friars. In the midst of this assembly Dominic arose, no longer merely Prior of a few Religious, but Master-General of an Order extending through the whole of Europe; holding his Chapter, not, as before, in a simple village church like that of Prouille, but in the very heart of a great and celebrated city, the rendezvous of the intellectual youth of many nations. No longer a source of anxiety to friends, his undertaking firmly established, Dominic at the age of fifty beheld himself surrounded by many able supporters, whose loss the universities did hot cease to regret.

The first proposal he made to the Chapter-General was the renunciation of all the property held by the Order, so that henceforth it should subsist only on daily alms. He had mentally formed this resolution long before, and from the time of the meeting at Prouille in the year 1216, the Friars had adopted it in theory, though not yet in practice. Dominic had always subsisted on charity since the momentous interview at Montpellier, from which time his apostolic labours date, as also his conviction that voluntary poverty was the only weapon by which heresy could be vanquished. Still there was a wide difference between a few missionaries and a whole Order subsisting on daily alms. All the traditions of the past seemed to discountenance so daring a step. From the time when she could hold any possessions, the Church made use of her riches, so that she might be independent of her enemies, liberal to the poor, and generous to her God. The very hermits of the East bought and sold, and gloried in earning their own living. Because riches had been abused, need they be entirely renounced? And supposing the world of that day stood in need of a striking example, would it be wise to make such an example a lasting one when the necessity for it might have passed away? Whether such reasons as these influenced Dominic, it is certain that he had accepted territorial possessions for his Order, with the intention of renouncing them at some future day. It is said that his intercourse with St. Francis of Assisi had inspired him with this idea, and it is certain that St. Francis had received from God the special mission to revive within the Church the love of poverty; but long before quitting all for Christ's sake, Dominic had traversed Languedoc, barefooted, clothed in a hair-shirt and an old mended tunic, trusting to Providence for his daily bread. During the fourth Lateran Council the two Saints, whose virtues had already edified the world, met for the first time in Rome, whither they had gone to solicit the approval of their Order's from Pope Innocent III. St. Francis of Assisi made instant choice of poverty as the patrimony of his Order. Dominic, not less austere as regarded himself, hesitated to impose the same observance on others until experience had proved the wisdom of his plan; then he renounced all the wealth acquired by his Order, which, with the consent of the whole Chapter, was ceded to the different Orders. A perpetual decree was made that for the future the Friars' sole treasure in this world should consist of their virtues. Dominic desired to go still farther, and leave the management of domestic matters entirely in the hands of the lay brothers, so that the others might give themselves wholly to prayer, study, and preaching. The Fathers of the Chapter opposed this, citing the recent example at Grandmont, where by a similar regulation the whole monastery had been left at the mercy of the lay brothers, and reduced to a state of degrading servitude. Dominic therefore yielded.

Other constitutions, still in force, were decreed by the Chapter-General, but we have no details regarding them. Dominic entreated the fathers to relieve him from the weight of government, saying, "I deserve to be deposed, for I am unprofitable and useless." [1] Apart from the feeling of humility by which he was prompted, he still desired to end his life among the infidels, and, in bearing them the truth, win the palm of martyrdom, which he had always so ardently longed for. More than once he expressed a wish to be scourged and hewn in bits for Christ's sake. In the effusion of his heart he one day

---

[1] *Actes de Bologne*, Rodolfo di Faënza's deposition, n. 4.

said to Friar Paolo di Venezia, "When we have regulated and formed our Order, we will go and preach to the Cumans, and win them for the Lord."[1]

This moment seemed now to have arrived. Had he not established the government and form of his. Order? Was it not there before his eyes as a flourishing vine? What better thing could he do than offer himself up as a living sacrifice? The fathers would not hear of his resignation; far from so doing, they confirmed his election as Master-General, which office he held with the approval of the Holy See. One thing Dominic obtained, which was that his power should be limited by certain officers named Definers, who during the holding of the Chapter should have the right of examining into and of regulating the affairs of the Order, and even of deposing the Master-General, should he betray his trust. This remarkable statute was afterwards approved by Innocent IV.

The Chapter separated after decreeing that it should reassemble annually, holding its sittings at Bologna and Paris alternately, excepting in the following year, when Bologna was to be again the meeting-place.

Of all European countries, Northern Italy was the one most tainted by heresy; her intercourse with the East and the baleful influence of the schismatic Emperors of Germany had made her swerve from her allegiance to the Church. Therefore Dominic resolved to evangelise it, and traversed the greater

---

[1] *Actes de Bologne*, deposition of Paolo di Venezia.

part of Lombardy during the summer of 1220. Contemporary historians record the fact, but give no
details. The majority of the Lombard towns claim
the honour of having received and listened to the
holy Patriarch, and their annals contain many anecdotes relative to his sojourn there; but they were not
written at the time, and their authenticity is not fully
proved. Certain it is that he visited Milan, and fell
sick there. Friar Bonvisi, who accompanied him in
this journey, thus describes his patience under suffering:—"When I was at Milan with Friar Dominic,
he had an attack of fever. I nursed him during his
sickness, and never heard him utter a complaint. He
gave himself to prayer and contemplation, and this I
knew by certain signs apparent on his countenance,
and which were familiar to me, inasmuch as I had
always remarked them whenever he prayed or meditated. As soon as the attack had passed, he began
discoursing with the Friars on the love of God; occupied himself with reading, or was read to; as was his
wont, he rejoiced more in affliction than in prosper-
ity."[1]

At Cremona Dominic met St. Francis of Assisi.
Whilst conversing together some Franciscans approached, saying, "We have no pure water in our
monastery, therefore we beseech that you, who are
our fathers and the servants of the Most High, will
intercede for us with the Lord that He may bless our
well, the water of which is thick and unfit to drink."

---

[1] Pierre Cali, *Vie de S. Dominique*, n. 21.

The two Patriarchs looked at one another, each expecting the other to reply; then Dominic said to the Friars, "Draw some water and bring it to us."[1] They obeyed, and Dominic addressed Francis in these words, "Father, bless this water in the name of the Lord." Francis replied, "Father, bless it yourself, for you are the greater."[2] This pious dispute went on for some time, until at last Dominic, yielding to Francis, made the sign of the Cross on the vessel, and commanded that its contents should be poured into the well, the waters of which were thenceforth pure.

A French Canon, *en route* for Rome, hearing Dominic preach at Modena, went to him at the close of the sermon and confessed that he was in despair as to his own salvation, and this on account of a temptation against chastity which he had been unable to overcome. "Take courage," replied the Saint; "trust in God's mercy, and I will obtain for you the gift of continence." The Saint fulfilled his promise.

When travelling, it was Dominic's wont to visit the monasteries which lay on his road. Among those where he stayed was that of Colombo in Parmesan, where the following incident is supposed to have taken place. Arriving at a monastery late one evening when the inmates had retired to rest, he, fearing to disturb them, lay down on the ground before the door with his companion, praying the Lord to provide for their necessities without awaking the monks. At the same instant they found themselves within the monastery.

---

[1] Le B. Humbert, *Vie de S. Dominique*, n. 51.

[2] Rodrigue de Cerrat, *Vie de St. Dominique*, n. 31.

Colombo was a celebrated Cistercian monastery founded by St. Bernard; it was destroyed by the Emperor Frederick II. in the year 1248.

That Dominic had returned to Bologna by the Feast of the Assumption is proved by the fact that Conrad the Teuton took the habit on that day. He was a Doctor in the University of Bologna, and so renowned for wisdom and virtue that the Friars ardently desired that he should be added to the number of those remarkable men who had joined their Order. On the Eve of the Assumption, Dominic was conversing familiarly with a Cistercian monk, who afterwards became Bishop of Alatri, but was at that time Prior of Casemare. Dominic knew him in Rome, and had conceived a warm affection for him; therefore, opening his heart that evening, he said, "Father Prior, I will reveal to you something that I have never yet mentioned to any one, and which I pray you to keep secret until after my death. It is this: God has never refused me anything that I have asked Him."

The Prior was greatly astonished at this, and knowing how anxious the Friars were to possess Master Conrad the Teuton, he replied, "If such is the case. Father, why do you not ask God to give you Conrad, whom the Friars are so desirous to have?" "My good brother," said Dominic, "what you ask me is very difficult to obtain; but if you will to-night join your prayers with mine, I am confident that the Lord will grant the favour you desire."[1] After Compline the servant of God remained in church, according to

---

[1] Le B. Humbert, *Vie de S. Dominique*, n. 50.

his usual custom, the Prior of Casemare being there also. They were present at the Matins of the Assumption, and at Prime, whilst the chanter was intoning *Jam lucis orto sidere*, Master Conrad entered the choir, and throwing himself at Dominic's feet, at once demanded the habit. The Prior of Casemare, faithful to his promise, never revealed the above incident until after the death of Dominic, whom he survived more than twenty years. He feared lest he might be summoned first, and mentioned this to the Saint, who assured him such would not be the case.

Among those whom Dominic received into the Order at that time was Thomas de Pouille, a young man of great purity and simplicity of manners, tenderly loved by the Saint, and styled his son. Some of the new Friar's former companions, angry at losing him, enticed him from the monastery and began tearing off his nlonastic dress. On learning this, Dominic at once went into the church to pray; and when the assailants, having robbed Friar Thomas of his woollen shirt, were endeavouring to clothe him in a linen one, their victim uttered lamentable cries, saying that he was burning; he would not rest until they led him back to the fold, robed in the rough and beloved garments of which they had stripped him. A similar thing happened to a jurisconsult of Bologna. His friends entered, armed, into the cloister of San-Niccolà in order to carry him off. The Friars wanted to oppose force to force, and for this purpose desired to fetch some knights who were friends of the Order, but Dominic said to them, "I behold around the church more than two hundred angels, whom the Lord has appointed to guard the Friars."[1]

The servant of God often preached in Bologna, where he was held in such veneration that the people, instead of awaiting him in the church, where he was to preach, met him at San-Niccolà and accompanied him to his destination. One day when the crowd had arrived in search of him, two students drew near, one of whom said to Dominic, "I pray you to beseech God to forgive me my sins, for I believe that I am penitent, and have made a full confession of them all." Dominic, who was still within the church, knelt before one of the altars, and, after praying a little while, returned to the young man, saying, "Take courage; persevere in the love of God, for He has forgiven all your transgressions." Then the other student, hearing these words, addressed the Saint saying, "Father, pray for me also, for I have confessed all my sins." Dominic again knelt at another altar and prayed. But on returning to the suppliant said, "My son, do not attempt to deceive God; your confession was not complete; you kept back one sin through shame." Then drawing him aside, told him what sin he had withheld. The student replied, "Father, you are right; pardon me."[2] Dominic conversed with him for some time and then set out with his escort.

This prophetic spirit was habitual with him. One day, meeting a Friar who was starting on a mission,

---

[1] Thierry d'Apolda, *Vie de St. Dominique*, ch. xvii. n. 209.
[2] Pierre Cali, *Vie de St. Dominique*, n. 18.

he stopped him, and, after a few moments' conversation, feeling inwardly convinced that this Friar was guilty of some transgression, interrogated him as to whether he had any money with him or no. The Friar humbly answering that he had, Dominic commanded him to throw it away instantly, and then imposed a penance, for he never allowed any fault to pass unpunished. Thierry d'Apolda says, "He was the first to observe the statutes of his Order, and did his utmost to ensure their observance by others. If through human weakness any Friar failed in this respect, Dominic did not spare him; but he so tempered severity by mildness that the punishment was received in the spirit in which it was intended. He did not reprove the transgressor at once, or allude to the fault until a fitting opportunity occurred, when he would say to the delinquent, 'Brother, on such and such an occasion you did wrong; glorify God and confess your sin.' Paternal in correction, he was tender as a mother to all in affliction. No speech more sweet or reassuring than his, and no mourner came to him who did not return comforted. He was as vigilant over the souls of his Friars as he was over his own soul, zealously watching over their progress in holiness and righteousness. And as it is written that *a man's gaity and the expression of his countenance, and the fashion of his garb bewray the character,* never could he endure to see any of the Friars deviate in dress from the strict poverty enjoined by the Rule. Unless any serious obstacle prevented, he preached or discoursed daily to the Friars, and that with such fervour, and amid such an abundance of tears, that his hearers were filled with deep compunction, none touching their hearts as he did."[1]

According to the same historian, there were three things which Dominic strictly enjoined upon his children: always to converse of God, or with God, to take no money with them on their journey, and not to accept any temporal possessions. He incessantly exhorted them to study, and to preach the Divine Word; he discerned if any had a talent for preaching, and could not endure such a one to be employed in any other work.

As is the case with all the Saints, Dominic had great power over Satan, and many times exorcised him from the Friars who were possessed. Sometimes the Prince of Darkness assumed various forms, in order to mar the Saint's meditation or to disturb him in his preaching. The following recital is borrowed from Thierry d'Apolda:—"One day when the Saint, as a vigilant sentinel, was keeping watch before the city of God, he encountered Satan prowling around the monastery like a wild beast. Stopping him, he said, 'Why prowlest thou thus?' The demon replied, 'Because of the prey.' Asked what he found in the dormitory, he answered, 'I rob the Friars of their sleep; I persuade them not to rise for their Office, and, when permitted, I send them dreams and illusions.' The Saint led him to the choir, asking him what he gained there. He replied, 'I make the Friars come in late, go out too soon, and I also disturb their devotions.' Interrogated as to the refectory, he said,

---

[1] *Vie de St. Dominique*, ch. xvi. n. 186 and 187.

'Who but eats more or less than is requisite?' When conducted to the parlour, he exclaimed, laughing, 'This is my territory; it is the scene of laughing, of foolish reports, and idle words.' But when taken into the Chapter, he tried to flee, saying, 'This place is an abomination to me; I lose here all that I gain elsewhere; here the Friars are warned of their faults; here they make self-accusations, do penance, and receive absolution.'"[1]

While traversing Lombardy, Dominic had seen many sad proofs of the decrease of faith. In several localities the ecclesiastical patrimony had been seized by the laity, every one pillaging the Church under the pretext that she was too rich. The clergy, reduced to a state of degrading servitude, could no longer fittingly provide for the celebration of divine worship, nor exercise the duty of almsgiving; and the sole means of justifying this spoliation was the perpetuation of the heresy to which it owed its birth. There can be no situation more dire for the Church than this. The goods she has lost, transmute their holders into her implacable enemies; heresy is a condition of their tenure; and time, which effaces all else, seems powerless to withstand this alliance of temporal interests and spiritual blindness.

As founder of a mendicant Order, Dominic had more right than others to oppose this fearful combination of evil. Therefore, to stem this, he instituted an association which he named the Militia of Jesus

---

[1] *Vie de St. Dominique*, ch. xv. 174 and 175.

Christ.[1]　It consistefd of men and women living in the world, who undertook to defend the liberty and property of the Church by every means in their power. They dressed as other people, save that their garments were of the Dominican colours, black and white; the former, symbolical of innocence, the latter, of penance. Although not bound by the vows of poverty, chastity, and obedience, they conformed their life as much as possible to the religious life, observing vigils, fasts, and abstinence, and reciting a certain number of Pater Nosters and Ave Marias in lieu of the Divine Office. They were authorised to elect a Prior of their own, and on stated days they assembled in a church belonging to the Order, to attend Mass and listen to a sermon. When Dominic had been canonised, the members of this association took the name of the *Militia of Jesus Christ and of the Blessed Dominic.* Later on, its militant character disappeared with the cause that gave it birth, and the association consecrated itself to the work of interior sanctification, under the appellation of *St. Dominic's Brothers and Sisters of Penance,* under which title it was confirmed and its rules modified by Munion de Zamora, seventh Master-General of the Order.　At different epochs Popes Gregory IX., Honorius IV., John XXII., and Boniface IX. granted

---

[1] Historians vary as to the epoch when this was founded. Some say it was during Dominic's sojourn in Languedoc; others, during his stay in Lombardy. We favour the latter opinion, which is supported by the most ancient record of the event. It is as follows:—"This scandal existed *in many places in Italy,* and grieved the holy Father Dominic, who had made choice of poverty."

it special privileges, and Pope Innocent VII. ap-
proved its Rule, as drawn up by Munion de Zamora.
The Bull is dated 1405, and was published in 1439 by
Eugenius IV.

The Militia of Jesus Christ was the Third Order
instituted by St. Dominic, or rather the third branch
of one single Order, embracing in its plenitude both
men and women of the world. By the institution of
Friar Preachers, Dominic had drawn monastic phal-
anxes from the desert, and girt them with the sword
of the apostolate. In forming the Third Order, he introduced religious life within the home; at the
hearth; and nuptial couch. The world beheld girls of
tender age, widows, married persons, and men of all
ranks, publicly wearing the insignia of a Religious
Order whose practices they observed in the privacy
of home. The spirit of association, so prevalent in
medieval times, favoured this movement. As one becomes a member of a family, country, or society, in
virtue of birth or promised service, so persons were
desirous to become members, of their own free will,
of those glorious bands serving Christ Jesus by
preaching and by penance. They donned the garb of
St. Dominic or St. Francis, grafting themselves on
one or other of those stems, that they might be nourished by its sap, though still retaining their own
individuality; they frequented the churches of the
Order; participated in its prayers; were united to it
by ties and deeds of friendship, and copied the virtues of its members as nearly as they could.
Retirement from the world was no longer considered
an absolutely necessary condition to leading a saintly

life; each chamber became a cell, each house a The-
baïd. When age, or the course of events, released the
Christian from his worldly duties, he then devoted
himself more fully to the cloister. If the death of wife
or child severed the ties which bound him to the
world, or revolution hurled him from his rightful
sphere and drove him into exile, another family was
waiting to welcome him to its embrace, another city
awaited him as its citizen; and, as youth conducts to
manhood, so he passed from the lowest Order to the
first. The history of this institution is most interesting. It has formed saints in every rank and condition
of life, and its numbers vie with those of the desert
and the cloister. Women, especially, have enriched
the Third Order with the treasure of their virtues.
Too often the unwilling bearers of a yoke imposed in
early childhood, the garb of St. Francis or St. Dominic enables them to escape from the tyranny to which
they are subjected. They could not seek the convent,
so the convent comes to them, and in some obscure
corner of the paternal or conjugal home they erect a
mysterious sanctuary, filled with the presence of the
Invisible Spouse, sole object of their love. Who has
not heard of St. Catherine of Sienna and St. Rose of
Lima, those two Dominican stars by which both hem-
ispheres have been illumined? Who but has read of
the Franciscan St. Elizabeth of Hungary? Thus God
aids His own, proportioning His miracles to their necessities; and, after having trained them in the
wilderness, he leads His people forth.

CHAPTER XVII.

St. Dominic's sixth and last journey to Rome—Second Chapter-General—The Saint's illness and death.

WITH the institution of the Third Order St. Dominic's work was accomplished. Nothing now remained to be done save to bid farewell to all he had loved on earth; and without doubt Rome was the spot he held most dear. Ere commencing his public life, he had journeyed thither with his earliest friend, Azévédo, and returned there to obtain the confirmation of his Order. In Rome he founded San-Sisto and Santa-Sabina, and made that city the centre of his Order. There he filled the office of Master of the Sacred Palace, won the confidence of two eminent Pontiffs, restored three persons to life, and became the object of an ever-increasing veneration. Rome was the seat of the Infallible Vicar of Him whom Dominic had ever loved and served. How could he close his eyes in death ere receiving once more the Papal benediction and gazing on those hills encircling the holy city? How fold his hands for their last rest ere offering the Holy Sacrifice once again on the altars of St. Peter and St. Paul? How take his last sleep until his feet had once more pressed the soil they had so often trod?

For a sixth time Rome welcomed to her maternal embrace that great man to whom she had given birth in her old age, that son who should raise up to her a faithful seed, even in lands as yet unknown. Honorius III. gave him many written proofs of his paternal affection and solicitude. In the first of these, dated 8th December 1220, he relieved several Friars from the irregularity they had incurred by their uncanonical reception of holy orders. In three other documents, dated 18th January, 14th February, and 29th March of the following year, he recommends the Friars to the whole of the Christian hierarchy. In another, of the 6th of May, he gave them permission to offer the Holy Sacrifice on a portable altar, in case of necessity. This was the last page Honorius signed in favour of the Order during its founder's life. This Pontiff had the singular privilege of beholding St. Dominic and St. Francis flourish during his reign, and his acts proved him not unworthy of this signal favour.

Whilst Dominic was paying his farewell visit to Rome, Providence sent him his earliest living friend, Foulques, Bishop of Toulouse. The sight of him recalled olden days in Languedoc, the erection of Notre-Dame-de-Prouille and Saint-Romain-de-Toulouse, together with all the blessings and memories that clustered around the cradle of the Order. How sweet must the converse of those two have been! God had crowned their mutual and secret vows by an unprecedented success; and the office of preaching, the necessity of re-establishing which they had so often discussed, was now exalted throughout the Church

by a Religious Order already extending from one end
of Europe to the other. Their share in this great work
awoke within them no feeling of pride, but their joy
in the Church's glory was the deeper for their previous sorrow at her woes. Foulques felt no regret that
God had chosen another to be the chief instrument in
carrying out His plan. From the very commencement
he had been superior to the secret sting of envy, and
his truly paternal soul rose above those fears so natural when another is at the helm. His crown was
pure, his heart content. And for Dominic, what more
could he desire? Oh, happy moment when the Christian, at the end of his course, filled with the happy
consciousness of having accomplished God's will,
shares the peace resulting from that holy service
with another Christian, his companion and his
friend!

One document extant owes its existence to this
meeting. It is a species of testament, the perusal of
which will console the reader for possessing no further details of their last intercourse.

"In the name of God, be it known to all who shall
read these lines, that for the remission of our sins,
for the defence of the Catholic faith, and for the welfare of the whole diocese, we, Foulques, grant to you
Dominic, MASTER OF PREACHING, to your successors,
and to the Friars of the Order, the church of Notre-
Dame-de-Fanjeaux, together with all tithes and
rights thereto pertaining, both those belonging to us
personally, and those appertaining to the church and
to the chaplain thereof; saving and except that we reserve to ourselves and to our successors the cathedral

rights, and the power of attorney, and also the cure
of souls, with which the priest presented to us by the
Master-General, by the Prior of the above church, or
by the Friars of the Order, will be invested. And we,
Dominic, MASTER OF PREACHING, in our own name
and in that of our successors and of the Friars of our
Order, cede to you, Foulques, Bishop, and to your
successors, the sixth part of the tithes of all the parish churches of the Toulouse diocese, which tithes
were formerly granted us by you, with the full consent of the Canons of St. Etienne. We renounce this
donation for ever, as well as our legal and canonical
rights thereto."[1]

This document is dated Rome, 17th April 1221.
Three seals are appended, those of the cathedral of
St. Etienne, Foulques, and Dominic. Dominic's seal
represents him standing dressed in the Friar
Preacher's garb and holding a staff; around it are engraved these words: "*Seal of Dominic, Minister of
Preaching.*" This proves that the lofty title of *Master
of Preaching*, attributed to him in the above deed,
was not his own choice, but was a homage on the part
of Foulques, who could find no words more fitted to
express the high esteem in which he held his friend.
In his Bulls and letters, the Holy Father always
styled Dominic, *Prior of Saint-Romain*, and later on,
Prior of the Order of Friar Preachers.

Foulques survived Dominic for the space of ten
years. He died on the 25th December 1231, and was

---

[1] In Mamachi, *Annales de l'Ordre des Frères Prêcheurs*, vol. i.
Appendix, p. 70.

interred in a chapel within the Abbey of Grand-Selve, not far from Toulouse. His tomb has disappeared beneath the existing ruins; but the lapse of ages and the vicissitudes of empires cannot efface the memory of an individual so intimately united with one over whose early career and destiny he has so faithfully watched, and by whose success he has been immortalised.

A few days after signing the above-named deed, Dominic set out from Rome by the Tuscan Road, on which route lay Bolsena, by one of whose inhabitants he had often been hospitably received, and who, during the Saint's life, was rewarded for such hospitality in the following miraculous manner. During a violent storm that ravaged the vineyard at Bolsena, Dominic was seen in the air extending his cloak over his host's vineyard, thus preserving it from the hail. This spectacle was witnessed by all the inhabitants, and Thierry d'Apolda mentions that, as late as the thirteenth century, the cottage where Dominic resided when passing through Bolsena was still to be seen in the vineyard. It was carefully preserved by the descendants of its former proprietor, in accordance with whose express recommendation the Friar Preachers always received a kindly welcome there. In the year 1221, Pentecost fell on the 30th May. It was the day fixed for the opening of the second Chapter-General at Bologna. On entering San-Niccolà, Dominic observed that they were raising the walls of one of the wings of the monastery in order to enlarge the cells. At seeing this he wept, saying to Friar Rodolfo, the procurator, and to the other Friars,

"How now! You wish to renounce poverty already, and build yourselves palaces!" He commanded that the work should be stopped, and it was not recommenced until after his death.

We know nothing of the doings of the second Chapter-General, save the division of the Order into eight Provinces, viz., Spain, Provence, France, Lombardy, Rome, Germany, Hungary, and England. Precedence was granted to Spain, not by virtue of antiquity, but out of respect for the holy Patriarch to whom she had given birth. Suéro Gomez was appointed Prior-Provincial of Spain; Bertrand de Garrigue, of Provence; Matthieu de France, of France; Jourdain de Saxe, of Lombardy; Giovanni di Piacenza, of Rome; Conrad le Teuton, of Germany; and Gilbert de Frassinet, Provincial of England. In the six first-named Provinces about sixty monasteries had been founded in less than four years. The two last, Hungary and Germany, having as yet received no Friar Preachers, Dominic at once dispatched members of the Order to those provinces.

Paul, destined for Hungary, was a professor of canon law in the University of Bologna, and had quite recently entered religion. He set out with four companions, among whom was Friar Sadoc, a man renowned for his great virtues. They founded their first monasteries in Vesprin and Albe-Royale, and later on advanced to the territory of the Cumans, so long the object of Dominic's solicitude, and amongst whom he desired to end his days. I shall relate but one incident in connection with the establishment of the Friars in Hungary; it will initiate us more fully

into the manner in which those holy undertakings
were accomplished. "In those days two Friars of the
Hungarian Province arrived at a certain village at
the hour of Mass. When Mass was ended and the
people had returned to their homes, the sacristan
closed the church door and the Friars remained outside, no one having offered them any hospitality.
Seeing this, a poor fisherman was moved by compassion, and yet dared not ask them under his roof,
having nothing to set before them. He ran home, saying to his wife, 'Oh, would that we had some food to
give those poor Friars! It grieves me to see them
standing there at the church door, and no one offers
them anything,' The woman replied, 'We have no
food at all, save a little millet.' Her husband nevertheless bid her shake the purse to see if there was
not something in it; she did so, and to their surprise
two pieces of money fell out. Transported with joy,
the fisherman said to his wife, 'Go quickly, buy some
bread and wine, and cook the millet and the fish.' He
then ran to the church, and finding the Friars still
there, humbly invited them to come home with him.
The Friars, seating themselves at that poor table
where so great love presided, appeased their hunger,
and after thanking their hosts, withdrew, praying
God to reward their entertainers. God heard their
prayer; and from that day the fisherman's purse was
never empty; there were always two pieces of money
in it. Its owner purchased a house, fields, sheep and
oxen; moreover, the Lord gave him a son. And not
until he was well provided for did the miracle of the

two pieces of money cease."[1]

The English mission was as successful as the Hungarian one. Gilbert de Frassinet, its head, presented himself and his twelve companions to the Archbishop of Canterbury, who at once ordered Gilbert to preach before him in a church, the pulpit of which he himself had intended to occupy that day. So pleased was he with the result, that he at once extended his friendship to the Friars, and remained their faithful protector till death. Their first establishment was at Oxford, where they erected a chapel, dedicated to Our Lady, and opened schools, named, after the parish in which they were situated, St. Edward's. Now that Dominic had established his Order in England and Hungary, the whole of Europe was his.

Ere long Heaven warned him of his approaching end. One day, while praying and longing for the dissolution of his earthly tenement, a young man of great beauty appeared, saying to him, "Come, my beloved, enter into bliss!"[2] The exact time of his departure was also revealed to him. And on visiting some of the university students of Bologna, to whom he was much attached, after conversing with them a while, he arose to take his leave, exhorting them to despise the world and remember the hour of death, adding, "Dear friends, now you see me in good health,

---

[1] Thierry d'Apolda, *Vie de St. Dominique*, ch. xxvii. n. 319, 320.

[2] Barthélemy de Trente, *Vie de St. Dominique*, n. 13.

but ere the Feast of the Assumption I shall have departed this mortal life."[1]

After this he started for Venice, to commend the interests of his Order once more to Cardinal Ugolino, then residing in Venice as Legate Apostolic, and also to take a lasting farewell of so dear a friend. It was the height of summer when he returned, arriving at the monastery of San-Niccolà one evening late in July. Though much fatigued by the journey, he conversed for a long while with Prior Rodolfo and Friar Ventura, the procurator, respecting the affairs of the Order. Towards midnight, the latter, being very tired, urged Dominic to retire to rest and not to rise for Matins. The Saint would not consent, but spent the night in prayer within the church, remaining there until the time of Office, which he celebrated with the Friars. After it was ended, he told Friar Ventura that he was suffering from headache; and, shortly after, violent dysentery set in, accompanied by fever. Though in great pain, he refused to go to bed, and only lay down on a woollen sack, dressed in his usual garb. The progress of the malady elicited no murmur, groan, or sign of impatience from the sufferer, who remained joyous as ever. But feeling that he was rapidly growing worse, he sent for the Friars, in whose presence he made a general confession to Friar Ventura. When it was concluded, he addressed them, saying, "Divine mercy has preserved my virginity unsullied to this day; if you desire the same grace, shun all dangerous intimacy.

---

[1] Gerard de Frachet, *Vie des Frères*, Bk. ii. ch. xxvii.

Chastity renders its possessor pleasing in the Lord's sight, and honoured and esteemed by man. Continue to serve God fervently; exert yourselves to maintain and extend this Order, which has only just begun; be steadfast in holiness, constant in obedience, and increase in all virtue."[1] Then, in order to rouse them to greater vigilance, he added, "Although Divine Goodness has hitherto kept me pure, I avow there is one imperfection I have not been able to overcome, that of taking more pleasure in conversing with young women than with aged ones."[2] Then, alarmed at his own sweet, saintly naïveté, he said in a low voice to Friar Ventura, "Brother, I think I have committed sin by speaking to the Friars publicly of my virginity; I ought not to have mentioned it."[3] Then turning to them again, bequeathed them the following legacy, saying: "My beloved brothers, this is the inheritance your Father leaves you; love one another, practise humility, and be faithful in the observance of voluntary poverty."[4] And in order to give greater force to the last clause of this testament, whoever should dare to corrupt his Order by bringing into it any worldly possessions, he threatened with God's malediction and his own.

The Friars did not yet despair of their Father's recovery, neither did they believe that God would so

---

[1] The Blessed Jourdain de Saxe, *Vie de St. Dominique*, ch. iv. n. 68.
[2] Ibid.
[3] Ibid.
[4] Ibid.

soon deprive the Church and themselves of his presence.   In compliance with medical advice, and
thinking that change of air might prove beneficial,
they removed him to Santa-Maria, a church situated
on an eminence near Bologna. But prayers and remedies were of no avail. Dominic grew worse, and
believing himself near death, summoned the Friars
anew. Twenty of them came with Ventura, their
Prior, and ranged themselves around the sick man.
Nothing has been preserved of the nature of Dominic's words on this occasion, save that never had
more touching, heartfelt utterances issued from his
lips. After this he received extreme unction. And
learning from Friar Ventura that the monk appointed to the church of Santa-Maria intended to
bury him there, he said, "God forbid that I should be
buried elsewhere than beneath the feet of my Friars.
Carry me out into the vineyard, that I may die there
and be interred in our own church."[1] Then the Friars
took him back to Bologna, fearing every moment that
he would expire in their arms. As he had no cell of
his own, they placed him in that of Friar Moneta.
They wished to change his garments, but having
none save those which he wore, Moneta gave one of
his own tunics with which to cover him.   Friar
Rodolfo supported the Saint's head, wiping the
death-sweat from his brow, the rest of the Friars
looking on, weeping. In order to comfort them, Dominic said, "Do not weep. I shall be of more use to you
where I am going than I have been here."[2] One of

---

[1] *Actes de Bologne*, Friar Ventura's deposition, n. 7.
[2] Ibid., Friar Rodolfo's deposition, n. 4.

the Friars asked him where he desired to be interred. He replied, "Beneath the feet of my Friars."[1] This was about an hour after their arrival in Bologna. Dominic observing that the Friars were so overwhelmed by grief that they were forgetting to pray for his departing soul, sent for Friar Ventura, telling him to "make ready."[2] They did so at once, and ranged themselves in solemn order around the dying man. He told them to "wait a while;" and Ventura, embracing this last opportunity spoke thus to the Saint: "Father, you know in what grief and desolation you leave us; remember us in the presence of the Lord."[3] Then Dominic, raising his eyes and hands to heaven, uttered this prayer: "Holy Father, I have accomplished Thy will, and those whom Thou hast given me I have kept; I now commend them unto Thee. Do Thou preserve and keep them."[4] And a moment after he told them to "begin."[5] They then commenced the solemn prayers for the departing soul, in which, from the movement of his lips, Dominic appeared to take part. When they came to these words, *"Let the holy angels of God come forth to meet him, and conduct him to the city of the Heavenly Jerusalem"* his lips moved for the last time; he raised his hands heavenwards, and God received his soul. This occurred at noon on Friday, 6th August 1221.

At the self-same day and hour. Friar Guala, Prior

---

[1] *Actes de Bologne*, Friar Rodolfo's deposition, n. 7.

[2] Ibid.

[3] Ibid.

[4] Ibid.

[5] Ibid.

of the monastery of Brescia, and afterwards Bishop of the same town, resting for a moment against the bell-tower of the monastery, fell into a light slumber, during which he beheld, in spirit, heaven open, and two ladders descending thence to earth. Above one was our Lord Jesus Christ, and at the summit of the other was His Blessed Virgin Mother. Between the two ladders, at their base, was placed a seat, on which was a person resembling a Friar, but his face being covered with a hood, after the manner of the dead, it was impossible to discern who he was. Ascending and descending the ladders were angels singing canticles. The ladders and he who was seated thereon, were drawn up by our Lord and His Blessed Mother, and when they had quite reached heaven, it closed, and the vision disappeared. Though still weak from the effects of recent illness. Friar Guala at once repaired to Bologna, where he learnt that Dominic's death took place on the very day and at the very hour in which he had seen the vision.

On the same day, two Friars living in Rome went to Tivoli, arriving there a little before noon. Tancred ordered his companion to say Mass, and on the latter making his confession, Tancred told him that as his penance he was to offer the Holy Sacrifice for their Father Dominic, then sick at Bologna. Reaching that part of the Mass where commemoration of the living is made, on directing his intention as enjoined, he fell into an ecstasy, during which he beheld Dominic leaving Bologna, having a golden crown upon his brow, surrounded with a brilliant light, and accompanied by two venerable persons, one on each side. It was also revealed to him at the same time that the servant of God had just expired, and had gloriously entered the celestial country. We have not far to seek for the meaning of the two ladders and the two aged persons. Doubtless they were typical of action and contemplation, those two things so marvellously combined by Dominic in himself and in his Order.

Providentially, Cardinal Ugolino arrived at Bologna shortly after Dominic had breathed his last. Desiring to celebrate the Funeral Office, he came to San-Niccolà, where the Patriarch of Aquilea, several Bishops, Abbots, nobles, and a number of persons had assembled. The body of the Saint was brought forth, spoiled of its sole remaining treasure, an iron chain, which had been worn next the flesh, and which Friar Rudolfo had removed on robing him in his grave-clothes. The chain was afterwards given by him to the Blessed Jourdain de Saxe. All hearts and eyes were riveted on that lifeless body. The Office commenced by mournful strains, partaking of the universal sadness, and falling like tears from the mourners' lips. By degrees the Friars raised their thoughts above this world; they no longer beheld their Father vanquished by death, leaving them only his lifeless remains. They were certain that he had entered glory; the funereal lamentations gave way to a song of triumph, and an unspeakable joy descended from heaven upon the hearts of all. At this moment, Albert, Prior of Santa-Caterina of Bologna, for whom

Dominic had cherished a warm affection, entered the church, and the joy of the Friars contrasting so vividly with his own deep sorrow, he could no longer restrain himself. Throwing himself on the lifeless body of the Saint, he covered him with kisses, holding him in a long embrace, as if to compel him to return to life and speak to him. His friend's remains responded to this deep love. Albert arose, saying to Prior Ventura, "Good news. Father Prior. Master Dominic has embraced me, and has told me that this very year I shall rejoin him in Christ."[1] He died within the year.

At the close of this Office, in which such intense grief and joy were so strangely blended, the Friars deposited their Fathers remains in a simple wooden coffin with long iron nails. He was placed there just as he was when he died, with no other perfume than the odour of his virtues. Beneath the pavement of the church a grave had been dug, the sides of which had been lined with thick stones. The coffin was let down, and re-covered with a heavy stone, carefully cemented, to guard it from the touch of rash hands. Nothing was engraved on this stone, neither was any monument erected. Dominic was, as he had desired to be, literally beneath his Friars' feet. On the night of his interment, a student of Bologna, who had been unable to be present at the funeral, beheld him in a dream in the Church of San-Niccolà seated on a throne and crowned with glory. Astonished at the sight, he said, "Did you not die. Master Dominic?"

---

[1] Gerard de Frachet, *Vie des Frères*, Bk. ii. ch. xxiii.

The Saint replied, "I am not dead, my son, because I have a Good Master, with whom I live."[1] On the following morning the student repaired to the Church of San-Niccolà and found Dominic's tomb on the very spot where he had beheld him seated on a throne.

Such in life and death was Dominic de Gusman, founder of the Order of Friar Preachers, a man endowed by nature with a most brilliant genius and most tender heart, gifts rarely combined in the same individual. The former manifested itself in the unceasing activity of his daily life, and the latter in that inner life of which it may be truly said, that each breath was an act of love to God and man. His contemporaries have bequeathed us brief but numerous records concerning him. Their perusal has filled me with admiration, so simple yet sublime is the spirit pervading them; it has filled me with astonishment on account of the character ascribed by them to their hero. For though I was certain that St. Dominic had been maligned by modern writers, I had no idea that history afforded so little warrant for their assertions. I have undeceived myself, and in so doing have learnt how difficult it is to preserve here below even a few vestiges of truth. What I have found I have faithfully recorded; but it was impossible to transcribe the deep love for Dominic with which these ancient writings overflow, nor yet the inexhaustible pleonasms with which the thirteenth century speaks of his gentleness, kindness, mercy, compassion, and all those

---

[1] Gerard de Frachet, *Vie des Frères*, Bk. ii. ch. xxix.

varying hues of which his loving heart was so susceptible. Their testimony is unimpeachable; they never
dreamt of writing from our point of view. If unable
to reproduce all the tenderness in my copy of their
portrait, I have at least learnt to blush at the mere
thought of transforming his history into an apology:
to do so would be to insult this great man, therefore
I close my record of his life, but proffer no defence. I
imitate his children, who graved no epitaph upon his
tomb, so persuaded were they that words were needless there. But as his earliest biographers, before
taking their leave of him, piously preserved the chief
traits of his physiognomy, I will do the same; and
though acknowledging my own inability to equal the
force and naïveté of their description, I will borrow
from the earliest and most illustrious of their number the venerated portrait of my Father.

The Blessed Jourdain de Saxe says:—"So pure
was he and so full of holy zeal, that at the first glance
one knew him to be a vessel of honour and grace, replete with precious gifts. Nought save compassion
and pity could alter the serenity of his soul. And because a contented heart makes glad the countenance,
the peaceful and happy expression of his features revealed the inner calm of his soul, over which no shade
of anger ever passed. He was resolute in his undertakings, and his words were well and carefully
weighed. His countenance, though radiant with
sweetness and amiability, commanded respect; yet
he easily won the hearts of all, even at first sight.
Whether journeying with companions, partaking of

hospitality at a stranger's table, or surrounded by nobles, princes, and prelates, it mattered not; wherever
he was, his conversation and example incited men to
the contempt of the world, and to the love of God. In
word and deed he was truly an apostolic man. By
day, when in the society of his Friars or with his companions, he was most winning and agreeable; by
night, he exceeded others in his vigils and his prayers. His tears he kept for evening, his joy for
morning; and knowing that God has set apart the day
for works of mercy, and night for prayer, he gave the
former to his neighbour and the latter to his God. He
wept much and often; tears were his food by night
and day, when offering the Holy Sacrifice, and also
during his nocturnal vigils. He rarely slept on a bed,
but passed his nights in church, watching and praying through the hours of darkness as long as his
bodily strength permitted, and when at last overpow-
ered by weakness, would take a short sleep in front
of the altar, or elsewhere, resting his head, like Ja-
cob, on a stone, and on awakening, would continue
his devotions. So wide was his charity that it embraced the whole human race, and as he loved all, so
was he beloved by all. He rejoiced with those who
rejoiced, and wept with those who wept, devoting
himself to his neighbour and to the afflicted. The
simplicity of his conduct made him universally beloved, so free was it from subtilty and guile. Being a
lover of poverty, he wore but mean garments; he kept
his body in subjection, observing great abstemious-
ness in eating and drinking, content with simple
food, moderate in the use of wine, taking only enough

to satisfy the needs of the body and yet leave his mind fresh and unclouded. Who shall ever equal this man's virtue? Admire him we may, and note how far he excels all others of our day; but attain his eminence in sanctity, that none can hope to do, save those privileged ones, if any such there be, to whom God shall vouchsafe His special grace to raise them to the same degree of holiness. Nevertheless, brothers, let us imitate our Father, as far as in us lies, and rendering thanks to the Redeemer in that He has given His servants such a guide, let us entreat the Father of Mercies that, aided by that Spirit by which His children are led, and following in the steps of our predecessors, we may enter by the narrow way into that blissful country whither the blessed Dominic has gone before." [1]

---

[1] *Vie de St. Dominique*, ch. iv. n. 74, &c

CHAPTER XVIII.

Translation and Canonisation of St. Dominic.

TWELVE years had elapsed since St. Dominic's death. God had manifested His servant's sanctity by numerous miracles wrought at his tomb or obtained by his intercession. Crowds of sick persons were constantly seen frequenting his resting-place, who after passing the day and night in its vicinity, went away healed, rendering thanks to St. Dominic for their cure. The surrounding walls were hung with *ex votos*, and time did but augment the veneration in which the Saint was held. But on the Friars' eyes a cloud seemed to rest; whilst their founder was exalted by the people, his children, far from cherishing his memory, seemed but desirous of dimming its radiancy. Not only did they leave his tomb devoid of ornament, but, lest they should be accused of seeking some personal advantage from the veneration of which their founder was already the object, they even removed the *ex votos* suspended from the walls. Such a mode of procedure was uncongenial to some of their number, who nevertheless did not venture to oppose their brethren. Finding their number constantly increasing, the Friars were compelled to pull down the old church of San-Niccolà in order to erect a new one, and the holy Patriarch's tomb was left unsheltered and expose to the rain and to the destructive influence of the seasons. Many of the Friars were so moved by this sight that they consulted together touching the removal of the precious relics to a more fitting resting-place; but they thought this could only be done with the authority of the Sovereign Pontiff. The Blessed Jourdain de Saxe expresses himself thus with regard to this point:—"Undoubtedly sons have the right of burying their father; but, in the exercise of this filial duty, God permitted them to seek the help of one far greater than themselves, so that the translation of the glorious Dominic should thereby be invested with a canonical character."[1]

So the Friars prepared a new tomb more worthy of their Father, and sent several of their number to consult with the Sovereign Pontiff. The venerable Ugolino Conti then filled the Papal throne under the title of Gregory IX. He gave the Friar a very cold reception, reproaching them for having so long neglected rendering due honour to their Father, adding, "I knew this truly apostolic man, and doubt not that in heaven he shares the glory of the Holy Apostles."[2] He even desired to be present at the translation; but as the duties of his office prevented his carrying this design into execution, he wrote to the Archbishop of Ravenna commanding him to proceed to Bologna in company with his suffragans in order to be present at the ceremony.

It was Pentecost in the year of grace 1233. The

---

[1] *Lettre Encyclique aux Frères*, in the *Actes des Saints*, by Bollandus, vol. i. August, p. 524.

[2] Ibid.

Chapter-General of the Order assembled at Bologna, and was presided over by the second Master-General, Jourdain de Saxe. In obedience to the Papal command, the Archbishop of Ravenna, and the Bishops of Bologna, Brescia, Modena, and Tournay were then present at Bologna. More than three hundred Friars from different countries had arrived. A large concourse of nobles and citizens of distinction from neighbouring towns crowded the different hostelries. All were full of expectation. "Nevertheless," says the Blessed Jourdain de Saxe, "behold the Friars in a state of extreme anxiety; they pray, grow pale, and tremble, fearful lest the Saint's body, so long exposed in its neglected tomb to the heat and the rain, should have become the prey of worms, and exhale an odour by which its reputation for sanctity should be diminished." [1] Tormented by this idea, they thought of opening the tomb in secret; but this God did not permit. Either suspecting their intention, or desirous of establishing more firmly the proofs of the authenticity of the relics, the Podestate of Bologna had the tomb guarded by armed knights. Nevertheless it was decided that, in order to secure more freedom of action, and also avoid the confusion that would result from the immense concourse of persons then present in Bologna, the tomb should be opened at night. Therefore, before daybreak on 24th May, two days after Pentecost, the Archbishop of Ravenna and the other Bishops, the Master-General of the Order, the

---

[1] *Lettre Encyclique aux Frères*, in the *Actes des Saints*, by Bollandus, vol. i. August, p. 524.

leading nobles and citizens of Bologna and of the neighbouring towns, assembled by torchlight around the lowly stone which for twelve years had covered St. Dominic's remains. In sight of all the spectators. Friar Stefano, Prior-Provincial of Lombardy, and Friar Rudolfo, aided by several other Friars, set about removing the cement in which the stone was laid. It was excessively hard, and offered much resistance, but having at last succeeded in overcoming this, the outer walls of the tomb became visible, Friar Rudolfo loosened the bricks by means of a hammer, and they were then able to remove the stone slab by aid of pickaxes, but this was not effected without much difficulty. On raising the stone, an indescribable perfume issued from the half-opened sepulchre, a perfume whose unimaginable fragrance was new to all. So astonished and delighted were the spectators, that they fell on their knees, weeping and praising God. The stone was then finally removed, and the wooden coffin enclosing the Saint's relics was beheld reposing within the vault. In the lid was a small opening through which the perfume issued abundantly, becoming yet more powerful with the removal of the coffin from the tomb. The knees of all were bent in veneration before that precious wood; they covered it with kisses and bedewed it with tears. At last they opened it by removing the nails in the lid, and the mortal remains of St. Dominic were revealed to his Friars and to his friends. There were only bones there, but bones whose celestial aroma bore witness to their glory and their life. No mortal can fathom the overflowing joy of the spectators; no mortal pencil portray the glories of that balmy night, the eloquence of that silence; those Bishops, knights, and Friars; those tearful faces of kneeling forms bending over a coffin, and seeking by the aid of torches to discern that great and holy man who beheld them from the heights of heaven, and who responded to their pious affection by those invisible embraces which fill the soul with overpowering bliss. The Bishops deemed their own hands not filial enough to touch the Saint's remains, and left that consolation and honour to his children. Jourdain de Saxe approached these holy relics with respectful devotion and removed them into a new coffin made of larix wood, which wood is said by Pliny to resist the effects of time. The coffin was closed by a triple lock, of which one of the keys was intrusted to the Podestate of Bologna, another to Jourdain de Saxe, and a third to the Prior-Provincial of Lombardy. The coffin was then borne to the chapel, where a plain marble tomb awaited it.

When the day arrived, the Bishops, clergy, Friars, and nobles reassembled within the Church of San-Niccolà, already thronged with a countless multitude, among which were persons of all nations. The Archbishop of Ravenna sang the Mass of the day, which was that of the Tuesday in Whitsunweek, and by a touching coincidence the Introit commenced as follows:—*Accipite jucunditatem gloriæ vestræ—Receive the joy of your glory.* A sublime fragrance, which the sweet clouds of incense could not overpower, issued from the open coffin; the blast of trumpets mingled from time to time with the chant of the priests and Friars; in the hands of the people shone a countless number of tapers, and ever the hardest heart yielded to the chaste raptures of that triumph of sanctity. The ceremony over, the Bishops deposited the closed coffin within the marble tomb, there to await in peace and glory the signal of the resurrection. But at the solicitation of several illustrious persons who had been unable to assist at the translation, the tomb was opened. Jourdain de Saxe, taking within his hands the venerated head of the holy Patriarch, presented it to more than three hundred Friars, who then had the consolation of touching it with their lips, which for a long space of time retained the perfume of that kiss. Whatever touched the Saint's relics became impregnated with their virtue. "We ourselves," says the Blessed Jourdain de Saxe, "have smelt this precious odour, and that which we have perceived we declare unto you. It seemed as if we never could satisfy ourselves with that fragrance, although we tarried for many hours near St. Dominic's remains. It never palled upon the senses, but excited the heart to piety; miracles were wrought by it, and the same odour was at once imparted to whatever touched the body, whether hand or girdle or any other object."[1]

With regard to this, Thierry d'Apolda says that during his lifetime God had vouchsafed the Saint this external mark of purity of soul. One feast day when celebrating Mass at Bologna, a student approached at the moment of the offertory and kissed the Saint's

[1] *Lettre Encyclique aux Frères*

hand. Now it so happened that this young man was victim to unchastity, from which, probably, he sought to be released. In kissing Dominic's hand he was conscious of a perfume that suddenly revealed to him all the honour and joy of the pure in heart, and from that moment he, by God's grace, overcame his corrupt propensities.

The striking miracles accompanying the translation of the Saint determined Gregory IX. to defer the canonisation no longer. By a letter of the 11th July 1233, the three following ecclesiastics were appointed to examine into the facts of the Saint's life, viz., Tancredo, Archdeacon of Bologna; Thomas, Prior of Santa-Maria-du-Rhin; and Palmeri, Canon of Santa-Trinita. The inquiry lasted from the 6th to the 30th of August. During this interval the nine following Friars—selected from the number of those intimately acquainted with St. Dominic—were sworn and their evidence heard. They were Ventura di Verona, Guillaume de Montferrat, Amison di Milano, Bonvisi di Piacenza, Jean de Navarre, Rodolfo di Faënza, Etienne d'Espagne, Paulo di Venezia, Frugeri de Penna. None of these witness having known St. Dominic in the early days of his apostolate, save Jean de Navarre, the Papal commissioners considered it necessary to form a second centre of inquiry in Languedoc, consisting of the Abbot of Saint-Saturninde-Toulouse, the Archdeacon of the same church, and the Archdeacon of St. Etienne. Twenty-six witnesses were examined, besides which, more than three hundred illustrious persons confirmed by oath and sign-manual all that the witnesses had deposed respecting St. Dominic's virtues and the miracles obtained by his intercession. The precise date of this document is not known, but it was near the end of 1233 or the commencement of the following year.

The depositions from Bologna and Toulouse having been forwarded to Rome, Gregory IX. deliberated thereon with the Sacred College. A contemporary author states that on that occasion the Holy Father, speaking of St. Dominic, said, "I no more doubt his sanctity than I do that of St. Peter and St. Paul"[1] The Bull of canonisation which was the result of these proceedings is couched in the following terms:—

"Gregory, Bishop, servant of the servants of God, to our venerable brothers the Archbishops and Bishops, to our dear sons the Abbots, Priors, Archdeacons, Archpriests, Deans, Provosts, and other Prelates of the Church whom these letters shall reach; health and apostolic benediction.

"The source of wisdom, the Word of the Father, whose essence is goodness, whose work is mercy, who redeems and regenerates those whom He has created, and who will tend the vine He has brought out of Egypt, even unto the end of the world, He, our Lord Jesus Christ, sends new signs and miracles, rendered necessary by the instability of men's minds and the daring attitude of unbelief. At the death of

---

[1] Etienne de Salanhac, *Desquatre choses en quoi Dieu a honoré l'ordre des Frères Prêcheurs.*

Moses, *i.e.*, at the close of the Old Testament dispensation, He mounts the four-horse chariot of the
Gospel, fulfilling the oaths sworn to our fathers, and
having in His hand the bow of Holy Writ, which He
kept bent during the Jewish times, He crosses the
waves of the sea to that vast extent of nations whose
salvation was prefigured in Rahab; He is about to destroy the pride of Jericho, the glory of the world, and
him whom in the sight of astonished nations He has
already conquered by the first sound of His voice.
The prophet Zacharias beheld four chariots come out
from the midst of two mountains of brass. In the first
were red horses, and by them are typified the rulers
of nations, the strong ones of the earth, who serving
by faith the God of Abraham, the father of the faithful, have, after his example, and in order to
strengthen the foundation of their faith, dyed their
garments in Bozra, that is to say, in the waters of
tribulation, and reddened all their standards with
their blood; these are they who, in view of the glory
to come, despised the temporal sword, and who, in
becoming martyrs, that is, witnesses, have by their
confession subscribed the book of the new law, added
to their confession the weight of miracles, consecrated the book and the tabernacles (the work not of
man but of God), and all the vessels of the gospel
ministry, not with the blood of animals, but with that
of human victims; and at last, by throwing the net of
preaching across the vast extent of seas, have drawn
within the Church of God all the nations under
heaven. But power having given rise to presumption
and liberty to license, the horses of the second chariot

were black, symbol of mourning and of penance.
They prefigured that battalion led by the Spirit of
God into the desert under the direction of St. Benedict, that new Elijah of the new Israel, that battalion
which restored to the children of the prophets the lost
treasure of community life, reunited the severed
links of unity, and by its good deeds extended itself
as far as that land of the north whence all evil proceeds, and gave to the contrite-hearted Him who
dwells not with the slave of sin. After this, as if to
refresh the wearied bands and give them joy for
lamentation, the third chariot appeared with white
horses, that is, with the monks of Cîteaux and of
Flore, who as sheep newly shorn, and full of the milk
of charity, issued from the bath of penance headed by
St. Bernard, that ram clothed with the Spirit of God,
who has led them into the thick of the valleys, so that
the passers-by, delivered by them, may cry mightily
to the Lord, hymn His praise, and pitch the camp of
the God of battles even on the very waves of the sea.
These are the three armies with which the new Israel
has defended herself from the equal ranks of the
Philistines.   But at the eleventh hour, when the
shades of night began to fall; when, because iniquity
abounded, the love of mercy grew cold, and the Sun
of justice was Himself nearing the horizon, the Lord
of the vineyard desired to assemble another army yet
more capable of protecting the vine that He had
planted, and which, although tended by many labourers hired at different seasons, had nevertheless
become encumbered with thorns and briars, and was
almost destroyed by a hostile number of little foxes.

Therefore, after the three first chariots, each with its
different symbols, God raised up in our sight, under
the figure of a fourth chariot drawn by strong horses
of another colour, the legions of the Friar Preachers
and Minorites, headed by leaders chosen for the combat. One was St. Dominic, a man endowed by God
with strong and ardent faith, whom, as His glorious
one, He sent forth on the divine mission of preaching.
Even in childhood he had a manly heart, practised
works of mortification, and walked in the presence of
God. Dedicated to God under the rule of St. Augustine, he resembled Samuel in his zeal for the house
of God, and David in the fervour of his holy desires.
As a courageous athlete he pursued the paths of
righteousness and the way of holiness, hardly ever
reposing from his spiritual labours, keeping his body
in subjection to his will, his senses in subjection to
his reason. Spiritually united with God, he strove by
contemplation to lose himself in the Divinity, and
this without neglecting works of mercy or diminishing his love for his neighbour. Whilst waging deadly
war against all sensuality, and illuming as with
lightning-flash the blinded minds of the impious, the
whole sect of heretics trembled and all the faithful
leapt for joy. He grew in grace even as he grew in
years, and so zealous was he for the salvation of
souls, that, not content with devoting himself wholly
to the work of preaching, he enlisted such numbers
beneath the same banner that he won a name and a
place among the Patriarchs. A prince and shepherd
among God's people, he instituted a new Order of
Preachers, guided it by his example, and confirmed

his mission by his miracles. For among the tokens by which his power and sanctity were manifested during his life, he restored hearing to the deaf and speech to the dumb, gave sight to the blind, restored the paralytic, and healed a multitude of sick persons. These miracles clearly revealed the spirit that animated his saintly frame. We who knew him intimately in the days when we filled a less exalted office in the Church, who saw in his life an evident proof of his sanctity, now that witnesses worthy of credit have attested to the truth of his miracles, we, together with the flock the Lord has intrusted to our care, believe that, thanks to the mercy of God, he may aid us by his suffrages, and after having consoled us on earth by his loving friendship, will aid us by his powerful patronage in heaven. Therefore, with the advice and consent of our brethren, and of all the Prelates at that time present, we have resolved to enroll him in the book of saints, and we decree and command you by these presents to celebrate his feast, and to cause it to be solemnly celebrated during the nones of August,[1] on the eve of the day on which he laid down the burden of the flesh, and entered, rich in merits, within the city of the saints, so that God, whom in life he honoured, moved by his prayers, may grant us grace now and glory hereafter. Desiring, moreover, that the tomb of this great confessor, by whose miracles the Catholic

---

[1] The Feast of St. Sixtus was on 6th August, and as the preceding day was dedicated to St. Mary ad Nives, St. Dominic's was fixed for 14th August.

Church is illumined, be worthily frequented and venerated by Christians. To the faithful who, having confessed their sins with sorrow, shall visit the tomb each year with respect and veneration on the Saint's feast-day, we grant an indulgence of a whole year, by virtue of the authority committed to us by God and by the blessed Apostles St. Peter and St. Paul. Given at Rieti, the 5th of the nones of July, in the eighth year of our Pontificate.[1]

With the exception of St. Hyacinth, Gregory IX. was the last survivor of the great men who had loved St. Dominic and aided in the completion of his designs. He died August 21, 1241, at the age of ninety-seven, having been for thirty years a Cardinal, and fourteen years a Pope. His personal qualities were neither eclipsed by the majesty of age nor the splendour of rank. A jurisconsult, a man of letters, a clever negotiator, not only was he endowed with every mental and physical gift, but with a noble soul large enough to contain St. Francis and St. Dominic, both canonised by him. It is not likely that we shall ever again see grouped around one single person such men as Azévédo, Montfort, Foulques, Reginald, Jourdain de Saxe, St. Hyacinth, Innocent III., Honorius III., and Gregory IX., nor so many virtues, nations, and events concur to bring about so mighty a result in so short a time.

With the Bull of canonisation the cultus of St.

---

[1] *Bullary of the Friar Preachers*, vol. i. p. 57. *Vide* also the Bollandists' *Commentaire préalable aux Actes de St. Dominique*, vol. i., August (5, 47), a dissertation regarding the date of this Bull, a date which has been the subject of some controversy.

Dominic spread throughout Europe; altars were erected to him in many places, but Bologna rendered herself conspicuous by her zeal for the great citizen bequeathed to her by death. In 1267 she removed the body from the unsculptured tomb where he reposed to a richer and more decorated one. This second translation was effected by the hands of the Archbishop of Ravenna, in presence of many other Bishops and of the Chapter-General of the Friar Preachers, and also of the Podestate and leading citizens of Bologna. The coffin was opened and the head of the Saint, after having been kissed by the Bishops and Friars, was exhibited to the people from a pulpit erected outside the Church of San-Niccolà. In 1383 the coffin was opened a third time, and the head placed in a silver urn, in order that the faithful might more readily enjoy the happiness of venerating that precious relic. On July 16, 1473, the marble tomb was again removed and replaced by one more highly sculptured, in the style of the fifteenth century. It was the work of Niccolò di Bari, and represents the different traits of the Saint's life. I shall not describe them. I have seen them twice, and twice, while on my knees gazing at them, the beauty of the tomb has convinced that a Divine Hand guided that of the artist, forcing the stone to express the incomparable goodness of that heart whose dust it covered. This glorious sepulchre has been untouched since then, and for three centuries no human eye has beheld the sacred remains which are interred there, nor even the wood of the coffin. The world was no longer worthy of such a sight. Dominic was conquered, at least,

as much so as it is possible for him to be who had
kept the battlefield for three hundred years. He too
is a victim to the ingratitude which deluded posterity
has showered on the men and the undertakings of
the Middle Ages, and must patiently wait in his
sealed and silent tomb for that justice which, on re-
flection, none can refuse to those who have laboured
on their behalf. Many of his contemporaries have
seen their statues reinstated by history. I am not so
sanguine as to the result of my efforts, but Time will
hold the pen when I am gone; and to Time I leave,
without fear or jealousy, the duty of completion.

NOTES

REGARDING THE EARLY RECORDS OF ST. DOMINIC'S LIFE.

1. *Du Commencement de l'Ordre des Frères Prêcheurs, par le Bienheureux Jordain de Saxe, deuxième Maître-général de l'Ordre.*—This is the earliest record of St. Dominic's life. That it was written before his translation and canonisation is proved by the author's silence on those points. It is therefore prior to the year 1233. It has been published with notes by Jacques Echard, the Dominican, in a work entitled *"Ecrivains de l'Ordre des Frères Prêcheurs,"* Paris, 1719. It was published a second time in 1773 by the Bollandists in the *Actes des Saints*, in the first volume for August, and is the edition from which we have quoted in this work.

2. *Lettre Encyclique aux Frères sur la Translation du Bienheureux Dominique, par le B. Jourdain de Saxe.*— This letter, the exact date of which is unknown, but which must have been written after the translation and before the canonisation of the Saint, that is, between the 24th May 1233 and the 3rd July 1234, is the complement of the preceding account. It was published by the Bollandists in the commentary preceding the Acts of the Saint.

3. *Actes de Bologne.*—These consist of the testimony of

nine of Dominic's disciples regarding the holy Patriarch's miracles and virtues. They are dated August 6 to August 30 in the year 1233, during which space of time the examination was going on. They have been published by Jacques Echard in the work already alluded to, also by the Bollandists in the *Actes des Saints*, and by Mamachi the Dominican in the Appendix to the first volume of the *Annales de l'Ordre des Frères Prêcheurs* printed in 1756. It is from the latter edition that our quotations are made.

4. *Actes de Toulouse.* — In these Acts twenty-six ecclesiastics and laymen bear testimony to the virtues and miracles of St. Dominic during his twelve years' sojourn in Languedoc. The precise date of these Acts is unknown, but they were of course anterior to the Saint's canonisation. They were published with those of Bologna in the three above-mentioned works. We have drawn our extracts from Mamachi's volume.

5. *Vie du Bienheureux Dominique, premier fondateur de l'Ordre des Frères Prêcheurs, par Constatin Medicis, Evéque d'Orviéto, du meme Ordre.*—This second account, which appeared between the years 1242 and 1247, was intended as complement to that written by the Blessed Jourdain de Saxe. It contains a few fresh details, but is far inferior both in style and matter. It was published by Jacques Echard.

6. *Vie du Bienheureux Dominique, par le B. Humbert, Maître-général de l'Ordre des Frères Prêcheurs.*—This is styled the third record, and appeared prior to the year 1254, in which year Humbert was elected Master-General. It is much more complete than the two others, and in order and style far superior to that of Constantin Médici. As St. Dominic's contemporaries were advancing in years and

their numbers diminishing, it is evident that the Blessed Humbert was anxious to record and preserve all he had learnt from them respecting this great man. His work was published by Mamachi in the Annals previously alluded to.

7. *Chronique de l'Ordre des Frères Prêcheurs, par le Bienheureux Humbert.*—This short but interesting chronicle of facts extends from 1202 to 1254, and is also included in Mamachi's work.

8. *Vie de St. Dominique, par Barthélemy de Trente, de l'Ordre des Frères Prêcheurs.*—This has been published by the Bollandists in their volume for August. It is an extremely short account, and dates from 1234 to 1251, but was not included in the number of the three leading records written in the interval between the years 1233 and 1254.

9. *Vies des Frères de l'Ordre des Prêcheurs, par Gerard Frachet, du même Ordre.*—This work was undertaken in compliance with the command of the Chapter-General held in Paris in 1256. They wished to preserve from oblivion some of the heroic deeds of the early days of the Order, which deeds occurred within the memory of aged persons still living.

Gerard de Frachet, a native of France and celebrated as a preacher, was commissioned by the Blessed Humbert, then Master-General, to collect these facts. He has done so in a work of exquisite and inimitable simplicity, which he entitled *Vies des Frères*, and divided it into four parts, the second of which relates to St. Dominic, but contains only a few isolated facts unrecorded in the previous Lives. The complete work was printed at Douay in 1619.

10. *Relation de la Soeur Cécile.*—Sister Cecilia, a member of the Cesarini family, was one of the nuns whom St. Dominic removed from the convent of Santa-Maria to that of San-Sisto. She was then seventeen years of age, and five years later she was appointed Prioress of Santa-Agnes-di-Bologna, where she lived until the year 1290, greatly renowned for her sanctity. Amongst the inmates of the same convent was one named Angelica, to whom Sister Cecilia specially confided all she had seen of St. Dominic during his residence at San-Sisto and Santa-Sabina. Sister Angelica wrote at Sister Cecilia's dictation. The narrative is written with naive simplicity, and is unequalled for the intimate knowledge it affords of the Saint's life. It concludes with these words: "S. Cecilia has related that which is here written concerning the B. Dominic ; she affirms that it is all so true that she will, if required, take an oath to that effect. But this precaution is needless, for so holy and religious is she that her veracity is unimpeachable; therefore S. Angelica of the convent of Santa Agnese has written down what she has received from her lips, that it may tend to the glory of our Lord Jesus Christ and that of our Blessed Father Dominic, and also be a consolation to the Friars. You who read, pardon the style, for he is not versed in grammar." This narrative, together with those of the Blessed Jourdain de Saxe, Constantin Médici, and the Blessed Humbert, are the four principal and earliest records of St. Dominic's life. The date is determined by the epoch at which Sister Angelica was living in the convent of Santa Agnese at Bologna; that is to say, about the year 1240. It was not much known till the end of the thirteenth century. It has been published by Mamachi.

11. *Vatican Chronicle.* — This also is contained in Mamachi's work; it is anonymous. It commences with the Saint's early life and closes in 1263.

12. *Des Sept Dons du Saint-Esprit, par Etienne de Bourbon, de l'Ordre des Frères Prêcheurs.*—The author entered the Order in the year 1219 and died in 1261. His work contains a number of facts concerning St. Dominic, and are taken from the records then in circulation.

13. *Le Bien Universel des Abeilles, par Thomas de Catimpré, de l'Ordre des Frères Prêcheurs.*—This book was published about the year 1261, and treats occasionally of St. Dominic and his Order.

14. *Miroir Historique, par Vincent de Beauvais, de l'Ordre des Frères Prêcheurs.*—Many chapters of this work are consecrated to St. Dominic. It was written about the same date as the preceding one.

15. *Vie du Bienheureux Dominique, par Rodriguez de Cerrat, de l'Ordre des Frères Prêcheurs.*—Rodriguez was born in Spain, in the valley of Cerrat, near Palencia, and flourished in the latter part of the thirteenth century. His work is but an imperfect compilation taken from the preceding ones. Its date is not precisely known, but it is after the year 1266, because it alludes to the monastery of Caralégua, founded by Alfonso the Wise in the house in which St. Dominic was born. This record is to be found in Mamachi's work.

16. *Vie de St, Dominic, par Thiérry d'Apolda, de l'Ordre des Frères Prêcheurs.*—The thirteenth century was nearing its close when Minion de Zamara, seventh Master-General of the Order, deemed it wise to mould into one all the various records, adding anything that had escaped the notice of the biographers. This task was intrusted to Thiérry d'Apolda, a German Dominican, a native of

Apolda, which lies between Jena and Weimar. In conformity with his General's orders, he issued in the year 1288 a new Life of St Dominic, much more voluminous than any other, and in which Sister Cecilia's narrative, which had till then remained in obscurity in the convent of Santa Agnese of Bologna, was published for the first time. This history is written lovingly, but not with much method, and its style, though less simple than that of the earlier historians, is not less devoid of vigour and grace. Thiérry d'Apolda is evidently the last of those who personally knew St. Dominic or his surviving disciples. He knew all that could be known respecting his hero; he gleaned the last ears of the harvest; and, in spite of the time that had elapsed and the inferiority of his style compared with that of Jourdain de Saxe, in his work we behold St Dominic's character faithfully portrayed, and without the slightest alteration. This Life has been printed by the Bollandists.

17. *Chronique de l'Ordre des Frères Prêcheurs, par Galvani della Fiammà.*—Galvani della Fiammà was born in 1283 and joined the Order in 1298. His Chronicle, though useful in some respects, has not been printed. The MS. is preserved in the Casanatese Library in the Monastery della Minerva in Rome.

18. *Des Quatre Choses en quoi Dieu a Honoré l'Ordre des des Frères Precheurs*, par Etienne de Salanhac, du même Ordre.—On account of the time in which Etienne de Salanhac flourished, he must be ranked among those biographers of the thirteenth century who immediately preceded Thiérry d'Apolda. He was born in 1210, and in 1230 received the habit of Friar Preacher from the hands of Pietro Cellani, and concluded his treatise about the year 1278. Unfortunately we do not possess this treatise in its original form, and this for the following reasons: — In

1304 Friar Aymeric di Piacenza having been elected Master-General of the Order in the Chapter-General held at Toulouse, commanded Bernardo Guidoni, a Dominican renowned for zeal and learning, to collect in one all the unpublished facts relative to the history of the Order. In a letter dated the same year, 1304, Bernardo gives his General an account of his researches. He makes mention, first of all, of having discovered Salanhac's treatise, to which, he says, he has added some things omitted by the author. He remarks at the commencement and at the close of the treatise that he has generally, but not invariably, written his additions on the margin. So that even if we possessed Salanhac's treatise as published by Bernardo Guidoni, the interpolations would prevent our distinguishing the work of either writer. But the negligence of the transcribers has much augmented this confusion. For in the existing MSS. of Salanhac's treatise the marginal notes indicating the majority of the additions have wholly disappeared. Therefore the treatise has lost its original value, and has no other authority than that it was found, annotated, and added to by Bernardo. In many parts it completely contradicts the records of the thirteenth century. It has never been printed, but a MS. copy exists in the Casanatense Library of La Minerva in Rome.

19. *Vie de St. Dominique, par Pietro Cali.*— This is a kind of rhapsody. The first twelve paragraphs are taken from Etienne de Salanhac's treatise, and the remaining ones are but a mass of unconnected. anecdotes. In the part copied from Salanhac the author has made even further additions. Pietro Cali wrote in 1324, more than a century after St. Dominic's death; this we learn from the twelfth paragraph of his book, where he speaks of Bernardo Guidoni's promotion to the See of Lodève, which promotion took place in 1324, under Pope John XXII.

Until the end of the fifteenth century St. Dominic had no new biographers, save a very few, and they only copied the Lives of the thirteenth century. We must, however, except Alain de la Roche, the Breton Dominican who altered all the traditions which till then had been preserved with such fidelity, and asserted that he wrote St. Dominic's Life by the aid of private revelations, citing authors whose names are unknown, and of whom no trace can be found. St. Antonio, Archbishop of Florence, who died in 1459, is the exact counterpoise to Alain de Roche, so carefully does he follow the text of the ancient records.

20. There are many portraits of St. Dominic, but it is difficult to decide as to their authenticity. We prefer the one at the commencement of this book. It is from the pencil of the Blessed Fra Angelico, the celebrated Dominican, who flourished in the early part of the fifteenth century. Fra Angelico held the Patriarch of his Order in high esteem and veneration; this is seen in all his delineations of the Saint; and it would seem beyond doubt that in portraying St. Dominic he followed the best authenticated representation of the Saint. This is evident by the perfect unity subsisting between all his portraits of St. Dominic. The one now given to the public is taken from the "*Crowning of the Virgin,*" a picture in the possession of France, and which is to be seen in the Louvre, in one of the galleries dedicated to the old masters.

CR
JESU

I am come to cast fire on the earth;
and what will I, but that it be kindled?
Luke xii, 49